Rubaiyat of Omar Khayyam
&
Salaman and Absal of Jami

Omar Khayyam and
Ralph Waldo Emerson
Translated By: Edward Fitzgerald

Rubaiyat of Omar Khayyam and Salaman and Absal of Jami

Copyright © 2022 Indo-European Publishing

The present edition is a reproduction of previous publication of this classic work. Minor typographical errors may have been corrected without note; however, for an authentic reading experience the spelling, punctuation, and capitalization have been retained from the original text.

ISBN: 978-1-64439-882-1

TABLE OF CONTENTS

TO E. FITZGERALD

Old Fitz, who from your suburb grange
Where once I tarried for a while,
Glance at the wheeling Orb of change
And greet it with a kindly smile;
Whom yet I see, as there you sit
Beneath your sheltering garden tree,
And watch your doves about you flit
And plant on shoulder, hand and knee,
Or on your head their rosy feet,
As if they knew your diet spares
Whatever moved in that full sheet
Let down to Peter at his prayers;

*   *   *

But none can say
That Lenten fare makes Lenten thought,
Who reads your golden Eastern lay,
Than which I know no version done
In English more divinely well;
A planet equal to the sun;
Which cast it, that large infidel
Your Omar: and your Omar drew
Full-handed plaudits from our best
In modern letters....

Alfred, Lord Tennyson

LIFE OF EDWARD FITZGERALD

Edward FitzGerald was born in the year 1809, at Bredfield House, near Woodbridge, Suffolk, being the third son of John Purcell, who, subsequently to his marriage with a Miss FitzGerald, assumed the name and arms proper to his wife's family.

St. Germain and Paris were in turn the home of his earlier years, but in 1821, he was sent to the Grammar School at Bury St. Edmunds. During his stay in that ancient foundation he was the fellow pupil of James Spedding and J. M. Kemble. From there he went in 1826 to Trinity College, Cambridge, where he made the acquaintance of W. M. Thackeray and others of only less note. His school and college friendships were destined to prove lasting, as were, also, all those he was yet to form.

One of FitzGerald's chief characteristics was what might almost be called a genius for friendship. He did not, indeed, wear his heart upon his sleeve, but ties once formed were never unloosed by any failure in charitable and tender affection on his part. Never, throughout a lengthy life, did irritability and erratic petulance (displayed 'tis true, at times by the translator of "that large infidel"), darken the eyes of those he honoured with his friendship to the simple and whole-hearted genuineness of the man.

From Oxford, FitzGerald retired to the 'suburb grange' at Woodbridge, referred to by Tennyson. Here, narrowing his bodily wants to within the limits of a Pythagorean fare, he led a life of a truly simple type surrounded by books and roses, and, as ever, by a few firm friends. Annual visits to London in the months of Spring kept alive the alliances of earlier days, and secured for him yet other intimates, notably the Tennyson brothers.

Amongst the languages, Spanish seems to have been his earlier love. His translation of Calderon, due to obedience to the guiding impulse of Professor Cowell, showed him to the world as a master of the rarest of arts, that of conveying to an English audience the lights and shades of a poem first fashioned in a foreign tongue.

At the bidding of the same mentor, he, later, turned his attention to Persian, the first fruits of his toil being an anonymous version, in Miltonic verse, of the 'Salámán and Absál' of Jámi. Soon after, the treasure-house of the Bodleian library yielded up to him the pearl of his literary endeavour, the verses of "Omar Khayyám," a pearl whose dazzling charm previously had been revealed to but few, and that through the medium of a version published in Paris by Monsieur Nicolas.

FitzGerald's hasty and ill-advised union with Lucy, daughter of Bernard Barton, the Quaker poet and friend of Lamb, was but short-lived, and demands no comment. They agreed to part.

In later life, most summers found the poet on board his yacht "The Scandal" (so-called as being the staple product of the neighbourhood) in company with 'Posh' as he dubbed Fletcher, the fisherman of Aldeburgh, whose correspondence with FitzGerald has lately been given to the world.

To the end he loved the sea, his books, his roses and his friends, and that end came to him, when on a visit with his friend Crabbe, with all the kindliness of sudden death, on the 14th June, 1883.

Besides the works already mentioned, FitzGerald was the

author of "Euphranor", a Platonic Dialogue on Youth; "Polonius": a Collection of Wise Saws and Modern Instances; and translations of the "Agamemnon" of Aeschylus; and the "Œdipus Tyrannus" and "Oedipus Coloneus" of Sophocles. Of these translations the "Agamemnon" probably ranks next to the Rubáiyát in merit. To the six dramas of Calderon, issued in 1853, there were added two more in 1865. Of these plays, "Vida es Sueno" and "El Magico Prodigioso" possess especial merit.

His "Rubáiyát of Omar Khayyám" was first issued anonymously on January 15th, 1859, but it caused no great stir, and, half-forgotten, was reintroduced to the notice of the literary world in the following year by Rossetti, and, in this connection, it is curious to note to what a large extent Rossetti played the part of a literary Lucina. FitzGerald, Blake and Wells are all indebted to him for timely aid in the reanimation of offspring, that seemed doomed to survive but for a short time the pangs that gave them birth. Mr. Swinburne and Lord Houghton were also impressed by its merits, and its fame slowly spread. Eight years elapsed, however, before the publication of the second edition.

After the passage of a quarter-of-a-century a considerable stimulus was given to the popularity of the "Rubáiyát" by the fact that Tennyson—appropriately enough in view of FitzGerald's translation of Sophocles' "Oedipus"—prefaced his "Tiresias, and other Poems," with some charmingly reminiscent lines written to "Old Fitz" on his last birthday. "This," says Mr. Edmund Gosse, "was but the signal for that universal appreciation of 'Omar Khayyám' in his English dress, which has been one of the curious literary phenomena of recent years. The melody of FitzGerald's verse is so exquisite, the thoughts he rearranges and strings together are so profound, and the general atmosphere of poetry in which he steeps his version is so pure, that no surprise need be expressed at the universal favour which the poem has met with among critical readers."

Neither the "Rubáiyát" nor his other works are mere translations. They are better, perhaps, described as consisting of "largely new work based on the nominal originals." In the "Omar," admittedly the highest in quality of his works, he undoubtedly took considerable liberties with his author, and introduced lines, or even entire quatrains, which, however they may breathe the spirit of the original, have no material counterpart therein.

In illustration of FitzGerald's capacity for conveying the spirit rather than the very words of the original, comparison of the Ousely MS. of 1460 A.D., in the Bodleian Library at Oxford, with the "Rubáiyát" as we know it, is of great interest.

The MS. runs thus:—

For a while, when young, we frequented a teacher;
For a while we were contented with our proficiency;
Behold the foundation of the discourse!—what happened to us?

We came in like Water, and we depart like Wind.

In FitzGerald's version the verses appear thus:—

Myself when young did eagerly frequent
Doctor and Saint and heard great Argument
But it and about: but evermore
Came out by the same Door as in I went.

With them the Seed of Wisdom did I sow
And with my own hand labour'd it to grow:
And this was all the Harvest that I reap'd—
"I came like Water, and like Wind I go."

Similar examples may be found elsewhere, thus:—

From the Beginning was written what shall be
Unhaltingly the Pen writes, and is heedless of good   and
bad;
On the First Day He appointed everything that   must
be,
Our grief and our efforts are vain,

develops into:—

The Moving Finger writes; and, having writ,
Moves on: nor all thy Piety nor Wit
Shall lure it back to cancel half a Line,
Nor all thy Tears wash out a Word of it.

The general tendency to amplification is shown again in
the translation of the two lines:—

Forsake not the book, the lover's lips and the green bank
of the field,
Ere that the earth enfold thee in its bosom.

into the oft-quoted verses:—

With me along some Strip of Herbage strown
That just divides the desert from the sown,
Where the name of Slave and Sultán scarce is known,
And pity Sultán Máhmúd on his Throne.

Here with a Loaf of Bread beneath the Bough,
A Flask of Wine, a Book of Verse—and Thou
Beside me singing in the Wilderness—
And Wilderness is Paradise enow!

And in the lines of Omar:—

In a thousand places on the road I walk, thou placest
snares.
Thou sayest: "I will catch thee if thou steppeth into them,"
In no smallest thing is the world independent of thee,

Thou orderest all things—and callest *me* rebellious!
majestically shaping into FitzGerald's rendering:—

Oh, Thou, who didst with Pitfall and with Gin
Beset the Road I was to wander in,
Thou wilt not with Predestination round
Enmesh me, and impute my Fall to Sin?

Oh, Thou, who Man of baser Earth didst make
And who with Eden didst devise the Snake;
For all the Sin wherewith the Face of Man
Is blacken'd, Man's Forgiveness give—and take!

To what school did FitzGerald belong? Who were his
literary progenitors? Lucretius, Horace and Donne, at any
rate, had a considerable share in moulding his thought
and fashioning the form of his verse. The unrhymed line,
so often but by no means uniformly resounding with a
suspended clangour that is not caught up by the following
stanza is distinctly reminiscent of the Alcaics of Horace.

Epicurean, in the ordinary sense of the term, he certainly
is, but it is of the earlier type. Cyrenaic would be a juster
epithet, the "*carpe diem*" doctrine of the poem is too gross
and sensual to have commended itself to the real
Epicurus. Intense fatalism, side by side with complete
agnosticism, this is the keynote of the poem. Theoretically
incompatible, these two "isms" are in practice inevitable
companions.

The theory of reincarnation and that alone, can furnish a
full explanation of FitzGerald's splendid success as a
translator.

Omar was FitzGerald and FitzGerald was Omar. Both
threw away their shields and retired to their tent, not
indeed to sulk, but to seek in meditative aloofness, the
calm and content that is the proper reward of those alone
who persevere to the end. Retirement brought them all it
could bring, a yet deeper sense of the vanity of things and

their unknowableness. Herein for the mass of mankind lies the charm of the Rubáiyát, in clear, tuneful numbers it chants the half-beliefs and disbeliefs of those who are neither demons nor saints, neither theological dogmatists nor devil-worshippers, but men.

Those seeking further information as to the life and place in literature of Edward FitzGerald are referred to Jackson's "FitzGerald and Omar Khayyám" [1899]; Clyde's "Life of FitzGerald" [1900]; Tutin's "Concordance to FitzGerald's Omar Khayyám" [1900]; and Prideaux's "Notes for a Bibliography of FitzGerald" [1901], and his "Life" [1903].

For an interesting discussion as to the real nature of Omar, see the Introduction to "Rubáiyát of Omar Khayyám" in the "Golden Treasury" Series.

W. S.

PREFACE TO
RUBAIYAT OF
OMAR KHAYYAM

Omar Khayyám, or Chiam, was born about the middle of the 11th Century, at Naishápúr, Khorassán, and he died in that town about the year 1123.

Little is known as to the details of his life, and such facts as are available have been drawn principally from the *Wasíyat* or *Testament* of Mizam al Mulk (*Regulation of the Realm*), who was a fellow-pupil of Omar at the school of the celebrated Imám Mowafek or Mowaffak. Reference to this is made in Mirkhond's *History of the Assassins*, from which the following extract is taken.

"'One of the greatest of the wise men of Khorassán was the Imán Mowaffak of Naishápúr, a man highly honoured and reverenced,—may God rejoice his soul; his illustrious years exceeded eighty-five, and it was the universal belief that every boy who read the Koran, or studied the traditions in his presence, would assuredly attain to honour and happiness. For this cause did my father send me from Tús to Naishápúr with Abd-u-samad, the doctor of law, that I might employ myself in study and learning under the guidance of that illustrious teacher. Towards me he ever turned an eye of favour and kindness, and as his pupil I felt for him extreme affection and devotion, so that I passed four years in his service. When I first came there, I found two other pupils of mine own age newly

1

arrived, Hakim Omar Khayyám and the ill-fated Ben Sabbáh. Both were endowed with sharpness of wit and the highest natural powers; and we three formed a close friendship together. When the Imám rose from his lectures, they used to join me, and we repeated to each other the lessons we had heard. Now Omar was a native of Naishápúr, while Hasan Ben Sabbáh's father was one Ali, a man of austere life and practice, but heretical in his creed and doctrine. One day Hasan said to me and to Khayyám, "It is a universal belief that the pupils of the Imám Mowaffak will attain to fortune. Now, if we *all* do not attain thereto, without doubt one of us will; what then shall be our mutual pledge and bond?" We answered, "Be it what you please." "Well," he said, "let us make a vow, that to whomsoever this fortune falls, he shall share it equally with the rest, and reserve no pre-eminence for himself." "Be it so," we both replied; and on those terms we mutually pledged our words. Years rolled on, and I went from Khorassán to Transoxiana, and wandered to Ghazni and Cabul; and when I returned, I was invested with office, and rose to be administrator of affairs during the Sultanate of Sultan Alp Arslán.'

"He goes on to state, that years passed by, and both his old school-friends found him out, and came and claimed a share in his good fortune according to the school-day vow. The Vizier was generous and kept his word. Hasan demanded a place in the government, which the Sultan granted at the Vizier's request; but, discontented with a gradual rise, he plunged into the maze of intrigue of an Oriental Court, and, failing in a base attempt to supplant his benefactor, he was disgraced and fell. After many mishaps and wanderings, Hasan became the head of the Persian sect of the *Ismaílians*,—a party of fanatics who had long murmured in obscurity, but rose to an evil eminence under the guidance of his strong and evil will. In A.D. 1090 he seized the castle of Alamút, in the province of Rúdbar, which lies in the mountainous tract, south of the Caspian sea; and it was from this mountain home he obtained that evil celebrity among the Crusaders, as the OLD MAN OF THE MOUNTAINS, and spread terror through the Mohammedan world; and it is yet disputed whether the word *Assassin*, which they have left in the language of modern Europe as their dark memorial, is derived from the *hashish*, or opiate of hemp-leaves (the Indian *bhang*), with which they maddened themselves to the sullen pitch of oriental desperation, or from the name of the founder of the dynasty, whom we have seen in his quiet collegiate days, at Naishápúr. One of the countless victims of the Assassin's dagger was Nizám al Mulk himself, the old school-boy friend.

"Omar Khayyám also came to the Vizier to claim his share; but not to ask for title or office. 'The greatest boon you can confer on me,' he said, 'is to let me live in a corner under the shadow of your fortune, to spread wide the advantages of Science, and pray for your long life and prosperity.' The Vizier tells us, that when he found Omar was really sincere in his refusal, he pressed him no further, but granted him a yearly pension of 1,200 *mithkáls* of gold from the treasury of Naishápúr.

"At Naishápúr thus lived and died Omar Khayyám, 'busied,' adds the Vizier, 'in winning knowledge of every kind, and especially in Astronomy, wherein he attained to a very high pre-eminence. Under the Sultanate of Malik Shah, he came to Merv, and obtained great praise for his proficiency in science, and the Sultan showered favours upon him.'

"When Malik Shah determined to reform the calendar, Omar was one of the eight learned men employed to do it; the result was the *Jaláli* era (so-called from *Jalal-ul-Din*, one of the king's names)—'a computation of time,' says Gibbon, 'which surpasses the Julian, and approaches the

3

accuracy of the Gregorian style.' He is also the author of some astronomical tables, entitled 'Zíji-Maliksháhí,' and the French have lately republished and translated an Arabic treatise of his on Algebra.

"These severe Studies, and his verses, which, though happily fewer than any Persian Poet's, and, though perhaps fugitively composed, the Result of no fugitive Emotion or Thought, are probably the Work and Event of his Life, leaving little else to record. Perhaps he liked a little Farming too, so often as he speaks of the 'Edge of the Tilth' on which he loved to rest with his Diwán of Verse, his Loaf—and his Wine.

"His Takhallus or poetical name (Khayyám) signifies a Tent-maker, and he is said to have at one time exercised that trade, perhaps before Nizám al Mulk's generosity raised him to independence. Many Persian poets similarly derive their names from their occupations: thus we have Attár 'a druggist,' Assár 'an oil presser,' etc. Omar himself alludes to his name in the following whimsical lines:—

"'Khayyám, who stitched the tents of science,
Has fallen in grief's furnace and been suddenly   burned;
The shears of Fate have cut the tent ropes of his   life,
And the broker of Hope has sold him for nothing!'

"We have only one more anecdote to give of his Life, and that relates to the close; related in the anonymous preface which is sometimes prefixed to his poems; it has been printed in the Persian in the appendix to Hyde's *Veterum Persarum Religio*, p. 449; and D'Herbelot alludes to it in his Bibliothéque, under *Khiam*:—

"It is written in the chronicles of the ancients that this King of the Wise, Omar Khayyám, died at Naishápúr in the year of the Hegira, 517 (A.D. 1123); in science he was unrivalled,—the very paragon of his age. Khwájah Nizámi of Samarcand, who was one of his pupils, relates the following story: "I often used to hold conversation with my teacher, Omar Khayyám, in a garden; and one day he said to me, 'My tomb shall be in a spot where the north wind may scatter roses over it.' I wondered at the words he spake, but I knew that his were no idle words. Years after, when I chanced to revisit Naishápúr I went to his final resting place, and lo! it was just outside a garden, and trees laden with fruit stretched their boughs over the garden wall, and dropped their flowers upon his tomb, so as the stone was hidden under them."'"

Much discussion has arisen in regard to the meaning of Omar's poetry. Some writers have insisted on a mystical interpretation and M. Nicholas goes so far as to state his opinion that Omar devoted himself "avec passion à l'étude de la philosphie des Soufis." On the other hand Von Hammer, the author of a *History of the Assassins*, refers to Omar as a Freethinker and a great opponent of Sufism.

Probably, in the absence of agreement amongst authorities, the soundest view is that expressed by FitzGerald's editor, that the real Omar Khayyám was a Philosopher, of scientific insight and ability far beyond that of the Age and Country he lived in; of such moderate and worldly Ambition as becomes a Philosopher, and such moderate wants as rarely satisfy a Debauchee; that while the Wine Omar celebrates is simply the Juice of the Grape, he bragged more than he drank of it, in very defiance perhaps of that Spiritual Wine which left its Votaries sunk in Hypocrisy or Disgust.

RUBAIYAT OF
OMAR KHAYYAM

I

Awake! for Morning in the Bowl of Night
Has flung the Stone that puts the Stars to Flight:
And Lo! the Hunter of the East has caught
The Sultán's Turret in a Noose of Light.

II

Dreaming when Dawn's Left Hand was in the Sky,
I heard a Voice within the Tavern cry,
"Awake, my Little ones, and fill the cup
Before Life's Liquor in its Cup be dry."

III

And, as the Cock crew, those who stood before
The Tavern shouted—"Open then the Door!
You know how little while we have to stay,
And, once departed, may return no more."

IV

Now the New Year reviving old Desires,
The thoughtful Soul to Solitude retires,
Where the White Hand of Moses on the Bough
Puts out, and Jesus from the Ground suspires.

V

Irám indeed is gone with all its Rose,

And Jamshýd's Sev'n-ring'd Cup where no one knows:
But still the Vine her ancient Ruby yields,
And still a Garden by the Water blows.

VI

And David's Lips are lockt; but in divine
High-piping Péhlevi, with "Wine! Wine! Wine!
Red Wine!"—the Nightingale cries to the Rose
That yellow Cheek of hers to incarnadine.

VII

Come, fill the Cup, and in the Fire of Spring
The Winter Garment of Repentance fling:
The Bird of Time has but a little way
To fly—and Lo! the Bird is on the Wing.

VIII

And look—a thousand blossoms with the Day
Woke—and a thousand scatter'd into Clay:
And this first Summer Month that brings the Rose
Shall take Jamshýd and Kaikobád away.

IX

But come with old Khayyám and leave the Lot
Of Kaikobád and Kaikhosrú forgot:
Let Rustum lay about him as he will,
Or Hátim Tai cry Supper—heed them not.

X

With me along some Strip of Herbage strown
That just divides the desert from the sown,
Where name of Slave and Sultán scarce is known,
And pity Sultán Máhmúd on his Throne.

XI

Here with a Loaf of Bread beneath the Bough,
A Flask of Wine, a Book of Verse—and Thou
Beside me singing in the Wilderness—
And Wilderness is Paradise enow.

XII

"How sweet is mortal Sovranty"—think some:
Others—"How blest the Paradise to come!"
Ah, take the Cash in hand and waive the Rest;
Oh, the brave Music of a *distant* Drum!

XIII

Look to the Rose that blows about us—"Lo,
Laughing," she says, "into the World I blow:
At once the silken Tassel of my Purse
Tear, and its Treasure on the Garden throw."

XIV

The Worldly Hope men set their Hearts upon
Turns Ashes—or it prospers; and anon,
Like Snow upon the Desert's dusty Face
Lighting a little Hour or two—is gone.

XV

And those who husbanded the Golden Grain,
And those who flung it to the Winds like Rain,
Alike to no such aureate Earth are turn'd
As, buried once, Men want dug up again.

XVI

Think, in this batter'd Caravanserai
Whose Doorways are alternate Night and Day,

8

How Sultán after Sultán with his Pomp
Abode his Hour or two and went his way.

XVII

They say the Lion and the Lizard keep
The Courts where Jamshýd gloried and drank deep:
And Bahrám, that great Hunter—the Wild Ass
Stamps o'er his Head, and he lies fast asleep.

XVIII

I sometimes think that never blows so red
The Rose as where some buried Cæsar bled;
That every Hyacinth the Garden wears
Dropt in its Lap from some once lovely Head.

XIX

And this delightful Herb whose tender Green
Fledges the River's Lip on which we lean—
Ah, lean upon it lightly! for who knows
From what once lovely Lip it springs unseen!

XX

Ah, my Belovéd, fill the cup that clears
To-day of past Regrets and future Fears—
To-morrow?—Why, To-morrow I may be
Myself with Yesterday's Sev'n Thousand Years.

XXI

Lo! some we loved, the loveliest and the best
That Time and Fate of all their Vintage prest,
Have drunk their Cup a Round or two before,
And one by one crept silently to Rest.

XXII

And we, that now make merry in the Room
They left, and Summer dresses in new Bloom,
Ourselves must we beneath the Couch of Earth
Descend, ourselves to make a Couch—for whom?

XXIII

Ah, make the most of what we yet may spend,
Before we too into the Dust descend;
Dust into Dust, and under Dust, to lie,
Sans Wine, sans Song, sans Singer, and—sans End!

XXIV

Alike for those who for To-day prepare,
And those that after a To-morrow stare,
A Muezzín from the Tower of Darkness cries,
"Fools! your Reward is neither Here nor There!"

XXV

Why, all the Saints and Sages who discuss'd
Of the Two Worlds so learnedly, are thrust
Like foolish Prophets forth; their Words to Scorn
Are scatter'd, and their Mouths are stopt with Dust.

XXVI

Oh, come with old Khayyám, and leave the Wise
To talk; one thing is certain, that Life flies;
One thing is certain, and the Rest is Lies;
The Flower that once has blown for ever dies.

XXVII

Myself when young did eagerly frequent
Doctor and Saint, and heard great Argument

10

About it and about: but evermore
Came out by the same Door as in I went.

XXVIII

With them the Seed of Wisdom did I sow,
And with my own hand labour'd it to grow:
And this was all the Harvest that I reap'd—
"I came like Water, and like Wind I go."

XXIX.

Into this Universe, and *why* not knowing,
Nor *whence*, like Water willy-nilly flowing:
And out of it, as Wind along the Waste,
I know not *whither*, willy-nilly blowing.

XXX

What, without asking, hither hurried *whence*?
And, without asking, *whither* hurried hence!
Another and another Cup to drown
The Memory of this Impertinence!

XXXI

Up from Earth's Centre through the Seventh Gate
I rose, and on the Throne of Saturn sate,
And many Knots unravel'd by the Road;
But not the Knot of Human Death and Fate.

XXXII

There was a Door to which I found no Key:
There was a Veil past which I could not see:
Some little talk awhile of Me and Thee
There seemed—and then no more of Thee and Me.

11

XXXIII

Then to the rolling Heav'n itself I cried,
Asking, "What Lamp had Destiny to guide
Her little Children stumbling in the Dark?"
And—"A blind Understanding!" Heav'n replied.

XXXIV

Then to the earthen Bowl did I adjourn
My Lip the secret Well of Life to learn:
And Lip to Lip it murmur'd—"While you live
Drink!—for once dead you never shall return."

XXXV

I think the Vessel, that with fugitive
Articulation answer'd, once did live,
And merry-make; and the cold Lip I kiss'd
How many kisses might it take—and give!

XXXVI

For in the Market-place, one Dusk of Day,
I watch'd the Potter thumping his wet Clay:
And with its all obliterated Tongue
It murmur'd—"Gently, Brother, gently, pray!"

XXXVII

Ah, fill the Cup:—what boots it to repeat
How Time is slipping underneath our Feet:
Unborn To-morrow and dead Yesterday,
Why fret about them if To-day be sweet!

XXXVIII

One Moment in Annihilation's Waste,
One Moment, of the Well of Life to taste—

The Stars are setting and the Caravan
Starts for the Dawn of Nothing—Oh, make haste!

XXXIX

How long, how long, in definite Pursuit
Of This and That endeavour and dispute?
Better be merry with the fruitful Grape
Than sadden after none, or bitter, Fruit.

XL

You know, my Friends, how long since in my House
For a new Marriage I did make Carouse:
Divorced old barren Reason from my Bed,
And took the Daughter of the Vine to Spouse.

XLI

For "Is" and "Is-not" though *with* Rule and Line,
And "Up-and-down" *without,* I could define,
I yet in all I only cared to know,
Was never deep in anything but—Wine.

XLII

And lately by the Tavern Door agape,
Came stealing through the Dusk an Angel Shape
Bearing a Vessel on his Shoulder; and
He bid me taste of it; and 'twas—the Grape!

XLIII

The Grape that can with Logic absolute
The Two-and-Seventy jarring Sects confute:
The subtle Alchemist that in a Trice
Life's leaden Metal into Gold transmute.

XLIV

The mighty Máhmúd, the victorious Lord
That all the misbelieving and black Horde
Of Fears and Sorrows that infest the Soul
Scatters and slays with his enchanted Sword.

XLV

But leave the Wise to wrangle, and with me
The Quarrel of the Universe let be:
And, in some corner of the Hubbub coucht,
Make Game of that which makes as much of Thee.

XLVI

For in and out, above, about, below,
'Tis nothing but a Magic Shadow-show,
Play'd in a Box whose Candle is the Sun,
Round which we Phantom Figures come and go.

XLVII

And if the Wine you drink, the Lip you press,
End in the Nothing all Things end in—Yes—
Then fancy while Thou art, Thou art but what
Thou shalt be—Nothing—Thou shalt not be less.

XLVIII

While the Rose blows along the River Brink,
With old Khayyám the Ruby Vintage drink;
And when the Angel with his darker Draught
Draws up to Thee—take that, and do not shrink.

14

XLIX

'Tis all a Chequer-board of Nights and Days,
Where Destiny with Men for Pieces plays:
Hither and thither moves, and mates, and slays,
And one by one back in the Closet lays.

L

The Ball no Question makes of Ayes and Noes,
But Right or Left as strikes the Player goes;
And He that toss'd Thee down into the Field,
He knows about it all—He knows—HE knows!

LI

The Moving Finger writes; and, having writ,
Moves on: nor all thy Piety nor Wit
Shall lure it back to cancel half a Line,
Nor all thy Tears wash out a Word of it.

LII

And that inverted Bowl we call The Sky,
Whereunder crawling coop't we live and die,
Lift not thy hands to *It* for help—for It
Rolls impotently on as Thou or I.

LIII

With Earth's first Clay They did the last Man's knead,
And then of the Last Harvest sow'd the Seed:
Yea, the first Morning of Creation wrote
What the Last Dawn of Reckoning shall read.

LIV

I tell Thee this—When, starting from the Goal,
Over the shoulders of the flaming Foal

15

Of Heav'n Parwín and Mushtara they flung,
In my predestined Plot of Dust and Soul.

LV

The Vine had struck a Fibre; which about
It clings my Being—let the Súfi flout;
Of my Base Metal may be filed a Key,
That shall unlock the Door he howls without.

LVI

And this I know: whether the one True Light
Kindle to Love, or Wrath consume me quite,
One Glimpse of It within the Tavern caught
Better than in the Temple lost outright.

LVII

Oh, Thou, who didst with Pitfall and with Gin
Beset the Road I was to wander in,
Thou wilt not with Predestination round
Enmesh me, and impute my Fall to Sin?

LVIII

Oh, Thou, who Man of baser Earth didst make
And who with Eden didst devise the Snake:
For all the Sin wherewith the Face of Man
Is blacken'd, Man's Forgiveness give—and take!

* * *

KÚZA—NÁMA
LIX

Listen again. One Evening at the Close
Of Ramazán, ere the better Moon arose,

16

In that old Potter's Shop I stood alone
With the clay Population round in Rows.

LX

And, strange to tell, among that Earthern Lot
Some could articulate, while others not:
And suddenly one more impatient cried—
"Who *is* the Potter, pray, and who the Pot?"

LXI

Then said another—"Surely not in vain
My substance from the common Earth was ta'en,
That He who subtly wrought me into Shape
Should stamp me back to common Earth again."

LXII

Another said—"Why ne'er a peevish Boy,
Would break the Bowl from which he drank in Joy;
Shall He that *made* the Vessel in pure Love
And Fancy, in an after Rage destroy!"

LXIII

None answer'd this; but after Silence spake
A Vessel of a more ungainly Make:
"They sneer at me for leaning all awry;
What! did the Hand then of the Potter shake?"

LXIV

Said one—"Folks of a surly Tapster tell,
And daub his Visage with the Smoke of Hell;
They talk of some strict Testing of us—Pish!
He's a Good Fellow, and 'twill all be well."

LXV

Then said another with a long-drawn Sigh,
"My Clay with long oblivion is gone dry:
But, fill me with the old familiar Juice,
Methinks I might recover by and bye."

LXVI

So while the Vessels one by one were speaking,
One spied the little Crescent all were seeking:
And then they jogg'd each other, "Brother! Brother!
Hark to the Porter's Shoulder-knot a-creaking!"

                          * * *

LXVII

Ah, with the Grape my fading Life provide,
And wash my Body whence the Life has died,
And in a Winding-sheet of Vine-leaf wrapt,
So bury me by some sweet Garden-side.

LXVIII

That ev'n my buried Ashes such a Snare
Of Perfume shall fling up into the Air,
As not a True Believer passing by
But shall be overtaken unaware.

LXIX

Indeed the Idols I have loved so long
Have done my Credit in Men's Eye much wrong!
Have drown'd my Honour in a shallow Cup,
And sold my Reputation for a Song.

LXX

Indeed, indeed, Repentance oft before
I swore—but was I sober when I swore?
And then and then came Spring, and Rose-in-hand
My thread-bare Penitence apieces tore.

LXXI

And much as Wine has play'd the Infidel,
And robb'd me of my Robe of Honour—well,
I often wonder what the Vintners buy
One half so precious as the Goods they sell.

LXXII

Alas, that Spring should vanish with the Rose!
That Youth's sweet-scented Manuscript should close!
The Nightingale that in the Branches sang,
Ah, whence, and whither flown again, who knows!

LXXIII

Ah, Love! could you and I with Fate conspire
To grasp this sorry Scheme of Things entire,
Would not we shatter it to bits—and then
Re-mould it nearer to the Heart's Desire!

LXXIV

Ah, Moon of my Delight who know'st no wane,
The Moon of Heav'n is rising once again:
How oft hereafter rising shall she look
Through this same Garden after me—in vain!

LXXV

And when Thyself with shining Foot shalt pass
Among the Guests Star-scatter'd on the Grass,

And in thy joyous Errand reach the Spot
Where I made one—turn down an empty Glass!

TAMÁM SHUD

SALAMAN
AND ABSAL

Jámi Noureddin Abdurrahman, Persian Poet, was born at
Jam, in Khorassán, in 1414. His best known poems are
"Yúsuf and Salikha," "Majnún and Laili," and "Salámán
and Absál." In addition to his poetry, he wrote a History of
the Sufí, and other prose works. He died in the year 1492.
FitzGerald's translation of "Salámán and Absál" in
Miltonic Verse was published anonymously in 1856.

I

PROLOGUE

Oh Thou whose Memory quickens Lovers' Souls,
Whose Fount of Joy renews the Lover's Tongue,
Thy Shadow falls across the World, and They
Bow down to it; and of the Rich in Beauty
Thou art the Riches that make Lovers mad.
Not till thy Secret Beauty through the Cheek
Of Laila smite does she inflame Majnún,
And not till Thou have sugar'd Shírín's Lip
The Hearts of those Two Lovers fill with Blood.
For Lov'd and Lover are not but by Thee,
Nor Beauty;—Mortal Beauty but the Veil
Thy Heavenly hides behind, and from itself
Feeds, and our Hearts yearn after as a Bride
That glances past us Veil'd—but ever so
As none the Beauty from the Veil may know.
How long wilt thou continue thus the World

21

To cozen with the Fantom of a Veil
From which Thou only peepest?—Time it is
To unfold thy perfect Beauty. I would be
Thy Lover, and Thine only—I, mine Eyes
Seal'd in the Light of Thee to all but Thee,
Yea, in the Revelation of Thyself
Self-Lost, and Conscience-quit of Good and Evil.
Thou movest under all the Forms of Truth,
Under the Forms of all Created Things;
Look whence I will, still nothing I discern
But Thee in all the Universe, in which
Thyself Thou dost invest, and through the Eyes
Of Man, the subtle Censor scrutinize.
To thy Harím Dividuality
No Entrance finds—no Word of This and That;
Do Thou my separate and Derivéd Self
Make one with Thy Essential! Leave me room
On that Diván which leaves no Room for Two;
Lest, like the Simple Kurd of whom they tell,
I grow perplext, Oh God! 'twixt "I" and "Thou;"
If I—this Dignity and Wisdom whence?
If Thou—then what this abject Impotence?

A Kurd perplext by Fortune's Frolics
Left his Desert for the City.
Sees a City full of Noise and
Clamour, agitated People,
Hither, Thither, Back and Forward
Running, some intent on Travel,
Others home again returning,
Right to Left, and Left to Right,
Life-disquiet everywhere!
Kurd, when he beholds the Turmoil,
Creeps aside, and, Travel-weary,
Fain would go to Sleep; "But," saith he,
"How shall I in all this Hubbub
Know myself again on waking?"
So by way of Recognition
Ties a Pumpkin round his Foot,
And turns to Sleep. A Knave that heard him

22

Crept behind, and slily watching
Slips the Pumpkin off the Sleeper's
Ancle, ties it round his own,
And so down to sleep beside him.
By and by the Kurd awaking
Looks directly for his Signal—
Sees it on another's Ancle—
Cries aloud, "Oh Good-for-Nothing
Rascal to perplex me so!
That by you I am bewilder'd,
Whether I be I or no!
If I—the Pumpkin why on You?
If You—then Where am I, and Who?"

Oh God! this poor bewilder'd Kurd am I,
Than any Kurd more helpless!—Oh, do thou
Strike down a Ray of Light into my Darkness!
Turn by thy Grace these Dregs into pure Wine,
To recreate the Spirits of the Good!
Or if not that, yet, as the little Cup
Whose Name I go by, not unworthy found
To pass thy salutary Vintage round!

II

And yet how long, Jámi, in this Old House
Stringing thy Pearls upon a Harp of Song?
Year after Year striking up some new Song,
The Breath of some Old Story? Life is gone,
And yet the Song is not the Last; my Soul
Is spent—and still a Story to be told!
And I, whose Back is crookéd as the Harp
I still keep tuning through the Night till Day!
That Harp untun'd by Time—the Harper's hand
Shaking with Age—how shall the Harper's hand
Repair its cunning, and the sweet old Harp
Be modulated as of old? Methinks
'Tis time to break and cast it in the Fire;
Yea, sweet the Harp that can be sweet no more,
To cast it in the Fire—the vain old Harp

That can no more sound Sweetness to the Ear,
But burn'd may breathe sweet Attar to the Soul,
And comfort so the Faith and Intellect,
Now that the Body looks to Dissolution.
My Teeth fall out—my two Eyes see no more
Till by Feringhi Glasses turn'd to Four;
Pain sits with me sitting behind my knees,
From which I hardly rise unhelpt of hand;
I bow down to my Root, and like a Child
Yearn, as is likely, to my Mother Earth,
With whom I soon shall cease to moan and weep,
And on my Mother's Bosom fall asleep.

The House in Ruin, and its Music heard
No more within, nor at the Door of Speech,
Better in Silence and Oblivion
To fold me Head and Foot, remembering
What that Beloved to the Master whisper'd:—
"No longer think of Rhyme, but think of Me!"—
Of Whom?—of Him whose Palace The Soul is,
And Treasure-House—who notices and knows
Its Incomes and Out-going, and *then* comes
To fill it when the Stranger is departed.
Whose Shadow—being Kings—whose Attributes
The Type of Theirs—their Wrath and Favour His—
Lo! in the Celebration of His Glory
The King Himself come on me unaware,
And suddenly arrests me for his own.
Wherefore once more I take—best quitted else—
The Field of Verse, to chaunt that double Praise,
And in that Memory refresh my Soul
Until I grasp the Skirt of Living Presence.

    One who travel'd in the Desert
    Saw Majnún where he was sitting
    All alone like a Magician
    Tracing Letters in the Sand.
    "Oh distracted Lover! writing
    What the Sword-wind of the Desert
    Undecyphers soon as written,

So that none who travels after
Shall be able to interpret!"—
Majnún answer'd, "I am writing
'Laili'—were it only 'Laili,'
Yet a Book of Love and Passion;
And with but her Name to dote on,
Amorously I caress it
As it were Herself and sip
Her presence till I drink her Lip."

III

When Night had thus far brought me with my Book,
In middle Thought Sleep robb'd me of myself;
And in a Dream Myself I seemed to see,
Walking along a straight and even Road,
And clean as is the Soul of the Sufi;
A Road whose spotless Surface neither Breeze
Lifted in Dust, nor mix'd the Rain to Mire.
There I, methought, was pacing tranquilly,
When, on a sudden, the tumultuous Shout
Of Soldiery behind broke on mine Ear,
And took away my Wit and Strength for Fear.
I look'd about for Refuge, and Behold!
A Palace was before me; whither running
For Refuge from the coming Soldiery,
Suddenly from the Troop a Shàhzemán,
By Name and Nature Hasan—on the Horse
Of Honour mounted—robed in Royal Robes,
And wearing a White Turban on his Head,
Turn'd his Rein tow'rd me, and with smiling Lips
Open'd before my Eyes the Door of Peace.
Then, riding up to me, dismounted; kiss'd
My Hand, and did me Courtesy; and I,
How glad of his Protection, and the Grace
He gave it with!—Who then of gracious Speech
Many a Jewel utter'd; but of these
Not one that in my Ear till Morning hung.
When, waking on my Bed, my waking Wit
I question'd what the Vision meant, it answered;

"This Courtesy and Favour of the Shah
Foreshadows the fair Acceptance of thy Verse,
Which lose no moment pushing to Conclusion."
This hearing, I address'd me like a Pen
To steady Writing; for perchance, I thought,
From the same Fountain whence the Vision grew
The Interpretation also may come True.

> Breathless ran a simple Rustic
> To a Cunning Man of Dreams;
> "Lo, this Morning I was dreaming—
> And methought, in yon deserted
> Village wander'd—all about me
> Shatter'd Houses—and, Behold!
> Into one, methought, I went—and
> Search'd—and found a Hoard of Gold!"
> Quoth the Prophet in Derision,
> "Oh Thou Jewel of Creation
> Go and sole your Feet like Horse's,
> And returning to your Village
> Stamp and scratch with Hoof and Nail,
> And give Earth so sound a Shaking,
> She must hand you something up."
> Went at once the unsuspecting
> Countryman; with hearty Purpose
> Set to work as he was told;
> And, the very first Encounter,
> Struck upon his Hoard of Gold!

Until   Thou   hast   thy   Purpose   by   the   Hilt,
Catch at it boldly—or Thou never wilt.

IV

THE STORY

A Shah there was who ruled the Realm of Yún,
And wore the Ring of Empire of Sikander;
And in his Reign A Sage, who had the Tower
Of Wisdom of so strong Foundation built

26

That Wise Men from all Quarters of the World
To catch the Word of Wisdom from his Lip
Went in a Girdle round him—Which The Shah
Observing, took him to his Secresy;
Stirr'd not a Step nor set Design a-foot
Without that Sage's sanction; till so counsel'd,
From Káf to Káf reach'd his Dominion:
No Nation of the World or Nation's Chief
Who wore the Ring but under span of his
Bow'd down the Neck; then rising up in Peace
Under his Justice grew, and knew no Wrong,
And in their Strength was his Dominion Strong.

The Shah that has not Wisdom in Himself,
Nor has a Wise Man for his Counsellor,
The Wand of his Authority falls short,
And his Dominion crumbles at the Base.
For he, discerning not the Characters
Of Tyranny and Justice, confounds both,
Making the World a Desert, and the Fount
Of Justice a Seráb. Well was it said,
"Better just Káfir than Believing Tyrant."

  God said to the Prophet David,—
  "David, speak, and to the Challenge
  Answer of the Faith within Thee.
  Even Unbelieving Princes,
  Ill-reported if Unworthy,
  Yet, if They be Just and Righteous,
  Were their Worship of The Fire—
  Even These unto Themselves
  Reap glory and redress the World."

V

One Night The Shah of Yúnan, as his wont,
Consider'd of his Power, and told his State,
How great it was, and how about him sat
The Robe of Honour of Prosperity;
Then found he nothing wanted to his Heart,

Unless a Son, who his Dominion
And Glory might inherit after him,
And then he turn'd him to The Shah and said;
"Oh Thou, whose Wisdom is the Rule of Kings—
(Glory to God who gave it!)—answer me;
Is any Blessing better than a Son?
Man's prime Desire; by which his Name and He
Shall live beyond Himself; by whom his Eyes
Shine living, and his Dust with Roses blows;
A Foot for Thee to stand on, he shall be
A Hand to stop thy Falling; in his Youth
Thou shall be Young, and in his Strength be Strong;
Sharp shall he be in Battle as a Sword,
A Cloud of Arrows on the Enemy's Head;
His Voice shall cheer his Friends to Plight,
And turn the Foeman's Glory into Flight."
Thus much of a Good Son, whose wholesome Growth
Approves the Root he grew from; but for one
Kneaded of Evil—Well, could one undo
His Generation, and as early pull
Him and his Vices from the String of Time.
Like Noah's, puff'd with Ignorance and Pride,
Who felt the Stab of "He is none of Thine!"
And perish'd in the Deluge. And because
All are not Good, be slow to pray for One
Whom having you may have to pray to lose.

      Crazy for the Curse of Children,
      Ran before the Sheikh a Fellow
      Crying out, "Oh hear and help me!
      Pray to Allah from my Clay
      To raise me up a fresh young Cypress,
      Who my Childless Eyes may lighten
      With the Beauty of his Presence."
      Said the Sheikh, "Be wise, and leave it
      Wholly in the Hand of Allah,
      Who, whatever we are after,
      Understands our Business best."
      But the Man persisted, saying,
      "Sheikh, I languish in my Longing;

Help, and set my Prayer a-going!"
Then the Sheikh held up his Hand—
Pray'd—his Arrow flew to Heaven—
From the Hunting-ground of Darkness
Down a musky Fawn of China
Brought—a Boy—Who, when the Tender
Shoot of Passion in him planted
Found sufficient Soil and Sap,
Took to Drinking with his Fellows;
From a Corner of the House-top
Ill affronts a Neighbour's Wife,
Draws his Dagger on the Husband,
Who complains before the Justice,
And the Father has to pay.
Day and Night the Youngster's Doings
Such—the Talk of all the City;
Nor Entreaty, Threat, or Counsel
Held him; till the Desperate Father
Once more to the Sheikh a-running,
Catches at his Garment, crying—
"Sheikh, my only Hope and Helper!
One more Prayer! that God who laid
Will take that Trouble from my Head!"
But the Sheikh replied: "Remember
How that very Day I warn'd you
Better not importune Allah;
Unto whom remains no other
Prayer, unless to pray for Pardon.
When from this World we are summon'd
On to bind the pack of Travel
Son or Daughter ill shall help us;
Slaves we are and unencumber'd
Best may do the Master's mind;
And, whatever he may order,
Do it with a Will Resign'd."

VI

When the Sharp-witted Sage
Had heard these sayings of The Shah, he said,

29

"Oh Shah, who would not be the Slave of Lust
Must still endure the Sorrow of no Son.
—Lust that makes blind the Reason; Lust that makes
A Devil's self seem Angel to our Eyes;
A Cataract that, carrying havoc with it,
Confounds the prosperous House; a Road of Mire
Where whoso falls he rises not again;
A Wine of which whoever tastes shall see
Redemption's face no more—one little Sip
Of that delicious and unlawful Drink
Making crave much, and hanging round the Palate
Till it become a Ring to lead thee by
(Putting the rope in a Vain Woman's hand),
Till thou thyself go down the Way of Nothing.
For what is Woman? A Foolish, Faithless Thing—
To whom The Wise Self-subjected, himself
Deep sinks beneath the Folly he sets up.
A very Káfir in Rapacity;
Clothe her a hundred Years in Gold and Jewel,
Her Garment with Brocade of Susa braided,
Her very Night-gear wrought in Cloth of Gold,
Dangle her Ears with Ruby and with Pearl,
Her House with Golden Vessels all a-blaze,
Her Tables loaded with the Fruit of Kings,
Ispahan Apples, Pomegranates of Yazd;
And, be she thirsty, from a Jewell'd Cup
Drinking the Water of the Well of Life—
One little twist of Temper,—all you've done
Goes all for Nothing. 'Torment of my Life!'
She cries, 'What have you ever done for me!'—
Her Brow's white Tablet—Yes—'tis uninscrib'd
With any Letter of Fidelity;
Who ever read it there? Lo, in your Bosom
She lies for Years—you turn away a moment,
And she forgets you—worse, if as you turn
Her Eye should light on any Younger Lover."

  Once upon the Throne of Judgment,
  Telling one another Secrets,
  Sat Sulayman and Balkís;

The Hearts of Both were turn'd to Truth,
Unsullied by Deception.
First the King of Faith Sulayman
Spoke—"Though mine the Ring of Empire,
Never any Day that passes
Darkens any one my Door-way
But into his Hand I look—
And He who comes not empty-handed
Grows to Honour in mine Eyes."
After this Balkís a Secret
From her hidden Bosom utter'd,
Saying—"Never Night or Morning
Comely Youth before me passes
Whom I look not longing after;
Saying to myself, 'Oh were he
Comforting of my Sick Soul!—'"

"If this, as wise Ferdúsi says, the Curse
Of Better Women, what should be the Worse?"

VII

The Sage his Satire ended; and The Shah
With Magic-mighty Wisdom his pure Will
Leaguing, its Self-fulfilment wrought from Heaven.
And Lo! from Darkness came to Light A Child
Of Carnal Composition Unattaint,—
A Rosebud blowing on the Royal Stem,—
A Perfume from the Realm of Wisdom wafted;
The Crowning Jewel of the Crown; a Star
Under whose Augury triumph'd the Throne.
For whose Auspicious Name they clove the Words
"Salámat"—Incolumity from Evil—
And "Ausemán"—the Heav'n from which he came—
And hail'd him by the title of Salámán.
And whereas from no Mother Milk he drew,
They chose for him a Nurse—her Name Absál—
Her Years not Twenty—from the Silver Line
Dividing the Musk-Harvest of her Hair
Down to her Foot that trampled Crowns of Kings,

31

A Moon of Beauty Full; who thus elect
Salámán of Auspicious Augury
Should carry in the Garment of her Bounty,
Should feed him with the Flowing of her Breast.
As soon as she had opened Eyes on him
She closed those Eyes to all the World beside,
And her Soul crazed, a-doting on her Jewel,—
Her Jewel in a Golden Cradle set;
Opening and shutting which her Day's Delight,
To gaze upon his Heart-inflaming Cheek,—
Upon the Darling whom, could she, she would
Have cradled as the Baby of her Eye.
In Rose and Musk she wash'd him—to his Lips
Press'd the pure Sugar from the Honeycomb;
And when, Day over, she withdrew her Milk,
She made, and having laid him in, his Bed,
Burn'd all Night like a Taper o'er his Head.

Then still as Morning came, and as he grew,
She dress'd him like a Little Idol up;
On with his Robe—with fresh Collyrium Dew
Touch'd his Narcissus Eyes—the Musky Locks
Divided from his Forehead—and embraced
With Gold and Ruby Girdle his fine Waist.—
So rear'd she him till full Fourteen his Years,
Fourteen-day full the Beauty of his Face,
That rode high in a Hundred Thousand Hearts;
Yea, when Salámán was but Half-lance high,
Lance-like he struck a wound in every One,
And burn'd and shook down Splendour like a Sun.

VIII

Soon as the Lord of Heav'n had sprung his Horse
Over the Horizon into the Blue Field,
Salámán rose drunk with the Wine of Sleep,
And set himself a-stirrup for the Field;
He and a Troop of Princes—Kings in Blood,
Kings too in the Kingdom-troubling Tribe of Beauty,
All Young in Years and Courage, Bat in hand

Gallop'd a-field, toss'd down the Golden Ball
And chased, so many Crescent Moons a Full;
And, all alike Intent upon the Game,
Salámán still would carry from them all
The Prize, and shouting "Hál!" drive Home the Ball.
This done, Salámán bent him as a Bow
To Shooting—from the Marksmen of the World
Call'd for an unstrung Bow—himself the Cord
Fitted unhelpt, and nimbly with his hand
Twanging made cry, and drew it to his Ear:
Then, fixing the Three-feather'd Fowl, discharged.
No point in Heaven's Azure but his Arrow
Hit; nay, but Heaven were made of Adamant,
Would overtake the Horizon as it roll'd;
And, whether aiming at the Fawn a-foot,
Or Bird on the wing, his Arrow went away
Straight—like the Soul that cannot go astray.

When Night came, that releases man from Toil,
He play'd the Chess of Social Intercourse;
Prepared his Banquet Hall like Paradise,
Summon'd his Houri-faced Musicians,
And, when his Brain grew warm with Wine, the Veil
Flung off him of Reserve. Now Lip to Lip
Concerting with the Singer he would breathe
Like a Messias Life into the Dead;
Now made of the Melodious-moving Pipe
A Sugar-cane between his Lips that ran
Men's Ears with Sweetness: Taking up a Harp,
Between its dry String and his Finger fresh
Struck Fire; or lifting in his arms a Lute
As if a little Child for Chastisement,
Pinching its Ear such Cries of Sorrow wrung
As drew Blood to the Eyes of Older Men.
Now sang He like the Nightingale alone,
Now set together Voice and Instrument;
And thus with his Associates Night he spent.

His Soul rejoiced in Knowledge of all kinds;
The fine Edge of his Wit would split a Hair,

And in the Noose of Apprehension catch
A Meaning ere articulate in Word;
His Verse was like the Pleiads; his Discourse
The Mourners of the Bier; his Penmanship,
(Tablet and running Reed his Worshippers,)
Fine on the Lip of Youth as the First Hair,
Drove Penmen, as that Lovers, to Despair.

His Bounty was as Ocean's—nay, the Sea's
Self but the Foam of his Munificence,
For it threw up the Shell, but he the Pearl;
He was a Cloud that rain'd upon the World
Dirhems for Drops; the Banquet of whose Bounty
Left Hátim's Churlish in Comparison—

IX

Suddenly that Sweet Minister of mine
Rebuked me angrily: "What Folly, Jámi,
Wearing that indefatigable Pen
In celebration of an Alien Shah
Whose Throne, not grounded in the Eternal World,
Yesterday was, To-day is not!" I answer'd;
"Oh Fount of Light!—under an Alien Name
I shadow One upon whose Head the Crown
Both Was and Is To-day; to whose Firmán
The Seven Kingdoms of the World are subject,
And the Seas Seven but droppings of his Largess.
Good luck to him who under other Name
Taught us to veil the Praises of a Power
To which the Initiate scarce find open Door."

Sat a Lover solitary
Self-discoursing in a Corner,
Passionate and ever-changing
Invocation pouring out;
Sometimes Sun and Moon; and sometimes
Under Hyacinth half-hidden
Roses; or the lofty Cypress,
And the little Weed below.

Nightingaling thus a Noodle
Heard him, and, completely puzzled,—
"What!" quoth he, "And you, a Lover,
Raving not about your Mistress,
But about the Moon and Roses!"
Answer'd he; "Oh thou that aimest
Wide of Love, and Lover's Language
Wholly misinterpreting;
Sun and Moon are but my Lady's
Self, as any Lover knows;
Hyacinth I said, and meant her
Hair—her Cheek was in the Rose—
And I myself the wretched Weed
That in her Cypress Shadow grows."

X

Now was Salámán in his Prime of Growth,
His Cypress Stature risen to high Top,
And the new-blooming Garden of his Beauty
Began to bear; and Absál long'd to gather;
But the Fruit grew upon too high a Bough,
To which the Noose of her Desire was short.
She too rejoiced in Beauty of her own
No whit behind Salámán, whom she now
Began enticing with her Sorcery.
Now from her Hair would twine a musky Chain,
To bind his Heart—now twist it into Curls
Nestling innumerable Temptations;
Doubled the Darkness of her Eyes with Surma
To make him lose his way, and over them
Adorn'd the Bows that were to shoot him then;
Now to the Rose-leaf of her Cheek would add
Fresh Rose, and then a Grain of Musk lay there,
The Bird of the Belovéd Heart to snare.
Now with a Laugh would break the Ruby Seal
That lockt up Pearl; or busied in the Room
Would smite her Hand perhaps—on that pretence
To lift and show the Silver in her Sleeve;
Or hastily rising clash her Golden Anclets

To draw the Crownéd Head under her Feet.
Thus by innumerable Bridal wiles
She went about soliciting his Eyes,
Which she would scarce let lose her for a Moment;
For well she knew that mainly by the Eye
Love makes his Sign, and by no other Road
Enters and takes possession of the Heart.

> Burning with desire Zulaikha
> Built a Chamber, Wall and Ceiling
> Blank as an untarnisht Mirror,
> Spotless as the Heart of Yúsuf.
> Then she made a cunning Painter
> Multiply her Image round it:
> Not an Inch of Wall but echoed
> With the Reflex of her Beauty.
> Then amid them all in all her
> Glory sat she down, and sent for
> Yúsuf—she began a Tale
> Of Love—and Lifted up her Veil.
> From her Look he turn'd, but turning
> Wheresoever, ever saw her
> Looking, looking at him still.
> Then Desire arose within him—
> He was almost yielding—almost
> Laying honey on her Lip—
> When a Signal out of Darkness
> Spoke to him—and he withdrew
> His Hand, and dropt the Skirt of Fortune.

XI

Thus day by day did Absál tempt Salámán,
And by and bye her Wiles began to work.
Her Eyes Narcissus stole his sleep—their Lashes
Pierc'd to his Heart—out from her Locks a Snake
Bit him—and bitter, bitter on his Tongue
Became the Memory of her honey Lip.
He saw the Ringlet restless on her Cheek,
And he too quiver'd with Desire; his Tears

36

Turn'd Crimson from her Cheek, whose musky spot
Infected all his soul with Melancholy.
Love drew him from behind the Veil, where yet
Withheld him better Resolution—
"Oh, should the Food I long for, tasted, turn
Unwholesome, and if all my Life to come
Should sicken from one momentary Sweet!"

> On the Sea-shore sat a Raven,
> Blind, and from the bitter Cistern
> Forc'd his only Drink to draw.
> Suddenly the Pelican
> Flying over Fortune's Shadow
> Cast upon his Head, and calling—
> "Come, poor Son of Salt, and taste of
> Sweet, sweet Water from my Maw."
> Said the Raven, "If I taste it
> Once, the Salt I have to live on
> May for ever turn to Loathing;
> And I sit a Bird accurst
> Upon the Shore to die of Thirst."

XII

Now when Salámán's Heart turn'd to Absál,
Her Star was happy in the Heavens—Old Love
Put forth afresh—Desire doubled his Bond:
And of the running Time she watch'd an Hour
To creep into the Mansion of her Moon
And satiate her soul upon his Lips.
And the Hour came; she stole into his Chamber—
Ran up to him, Life's offer in her Hand—
And, falling like a Shadow at his Feet,
She laid her Face beneath. Salámán then
With all the Courtesies of Princely Grace
Put forth his Hand—he rais'd her in his Arms—
He held her trembling there—and from that Fount
Drew first Desire; then Deeper from her Lips,
That, yielding, mutually drew from his
A Wine that ever drawn from never fail'd—

37

So through the Day—so through another still—
The Day became a Seventh—the Seventh a Moon—
The Moon a Year—while they rejoiced together,
Thinking their pleasure never was to end.
But rolling Heaven whisper'd from his Ambush,
"So in my License is it not set down.
Ah for the sweet Societies I make
At Morning and before the Nightfall break;
Ah for the Bliss that with the Setting Sun
I mix, and, with his Rising, all is done!"

> Into Bagdad came a hungry
> Arab—after many days of waiting
> In to the Khalífah's Supper
> Push'd, and got before a Pasty
> Luscious as the Lip of Beauty,
> Or the Tongue of Eloquence.
> Soon as seen, Indecent Hunger
> Seizes up and swallows down;
> Then his mouth undaunted wiping—
> "Oh Khalífah, hear me Swear,
> Not of any other Pasty
> Than of Thine to sup or dine."
> The Khalífah laugh'd and answer'd;
> "Fool; who thinkest to determine
> What is in the Hands of Fate—
> Take and thrust him from the Gate!"

XIII

While a Full Year was counted by the Moon,
Salámán and Absál rejoiced together,
And for so long he stood not in the face
Of Sage or Shah, and their bereavéd Hearts
Were torn in twain with the Desire of Him.
They question'd those about him, and from them
Heard something; then Himself in Presence summon'd,
And, subtly sifting on all sides, so plied
Interrogation till it hit the Mark,
And all the Truth was told. Then Sage and Shah

Struck out with Hand and Foot in his Redress.
And First with Reason, which is also Best;
Reason that rights the Retrograde—completes
The Imperfect—Reason that unties the Knot:
For Reason is the Fountain from of old
From which the Prophets drew, and none beside.
Who boasts of other Inspiration lies—
There are no other Prophets than The Wise.

XIV

First spoke The Shah;—"Salámán, Oh my Soul,
Oh Taper of the Banquet of my House,
Light of the Eyes of my Prosperity,
And making bloom the Court of Hope with Rose;
Years Rose-bud-like my own Blood I devour'd
Till in my hand I carried thee, my Rose;
Oh do not tear my Garment from my Hand,
Nor wound thy Father with a Dagger Thorn.
Years for thy sake the Crown has worn my Brow,
And Years my Foot been growing to the Throne
Only for Thee—Oh spurn them not with Thine;
Oh turn thy Face from Dalliance unwise,
Lay not thy Heart's hand on a Minion!
For what thy Proper Pastime? Is it not
To mount and manage Rakhsh along the Field;
Not, with no stouter weapon than a Love-lock,
Idly reclining on a Silver Breast.
Go, fly thine Arrow at the Antelope
And Lion—let not me my Lion see
Slain by the Arrow eyes of a Ghazál.
Go, flash thy Steel among the Ranks of Men,
And smite the Warriors' Necks; not, flying them,
Lay down thine own beneath a Woman's Foot,
Leave off such doing in the Name of God,
Nor bring thy Father weeping to the Ground;
Years have I held myself aloft, and all
For Thee—Oh Shame if thou prepare my Fall!"

When before Shirúeh's Feet

Drencht in Blood fell Kai Khusrau,
He declared this Parable—
"Wretch!—There was a Branch that, waxing
Wanton o'er the Root he drank from,
At a Draught the Living Water
Drain'd wherewith Himself to crown!
Died the Root—and with it died
The Branch—and barren was brought down!"

XV

Salámán heard—the Sea of his Soul was mov'd,
And bubbled up with Jewels, and he said;
"Oh Shah, I am the Slave of thy Desire,
Dust of thy Throne ascending Foot am I;
Whatever thou Desirest I would do,
But sicken of my own Incompetence;
Not in the Hand of my infirmer Will
To carry into Deed mine own Desire.
Time upon Time I torture mine own Soul,
Devising liberation from the Snare
I languish in. But when upon that Moon
I *think*, my Soul relapses—and when *look*—
I leave both Worlds behind to follow her!"

XVI

The Shah ceased Counsel, and the Sage began.
"Oh Thou new Vintage of a Garden old,
Last Blazon of the Pen of 'Let There Be,'
Who read'st the Seven and Four; interpretest
The writing on the Leaves of Night and Day—
Archetype of the Assembly of the World,
Who hold'st the Key of Adam's Treasury—
(Know thine own Dignity and slight it not,
For Thou art Greater yet than all I tell)—
The Mighty Hand that mix'd thy Dust inscribed
The Character of Wisdom on thy Heart;
O Cleanse Thy Bosom of Material Form,
And turn the Mirror of the Soul to Spirit,

40

Until it be with Spirit all possest,
Drown'd in the Light of Intellectual Truth.
Oh veil thine Eyes from Mortal Paramour,
And follow not her Step!—For what is She?—
What is She but a Vice and a Reproach,
Her very Garment-hem Pollution!
For such Pollution madden not thine Eyes,
Waste not thy Body's Strength, nor taint thy Soul,
Nor set the Body and the Soul in Strife!
Supreme is thine Original Degree,
Thy Star upon the Top of Heaven; but Lust
Will fling it down even unto the Dust!"

> Quoth a Muezzin unto Crested
> Chanticleer—"Oh Voice of Morning,
> Not a Sage of all the Sages
> Prophesies of Dawn, or startles
> At the wing of Time, like Thee.
> One so wise methinks were fitter
> Perching on the Beams of Heaven,
> Than with those poor Hens about him,
> Raking in a Heap of Dung."
> "And," replied the Cock, "in Heaven
> Once I was; but by my Evil
> Lust am fallen down to raking
> With my wretched Hens about me
> On the Dunghill. Otherwise
> I were even now in Eden
> With the Bird of Paradise."

XVII

When from The Sage these words Salámán heard,
The breath of Wisdom round his Palate blew;
He said—"Oh Darling of the Soul of Plato,
To whom a hundred Aristotles bow;
Oh Thou that an Eleventh to the Ten
Original Intelligences addest,—
I lay my Face before Thee in the Dust,
The humblest Scholar of thy Court am I;

41

Whose every word I find a Well of Wisdom,
And hasten to imbibe it in my Soul.
But clear unto thy clearest Eye it is,
That Choice is not within Oneself—To Do,
Not in The Will, but in The Power, to Do.
From that which I originally am
How shall I swerve? or how put forth a Sign
Beyond the Power that is by Nature Mine?"

XVIII

Unto the Soul that is confused by Love
Comes Sorrow after Sorrow—most of all
To Love whose only Friendship is Reproof,
And overmuch of Counsel—whereby Love
Grows stubborn, and increases the Disease.
Love unreproved is a delicious food;
Reproved, is Feeding on one's own Heart's Blood.
Salámán heard; his Soul came to his Lips;
Reproaches struck not Absál out of him,
But drove Confusion in; bitter became
The Drinking of the sweet Draught of Delight,
And wan'd the Splendour of his Moon of Beauty.
His Breath was Indignation, and his Heart
Bled from the Arrow, and his Anguish grew—
How bear it?—Able to endure one wound,
From Wound on Wound no remedy but Flight;
Day after Day, Design upon Design,
He turn'd the Matter over in his Heart,
And, after all, no Remedy but Flight.
Resolv'd on that, he victuall'd and equipp'd
A Camel, and one Night he led it forth,
And mounted—he and Absál at his side,
The fair Salámán and Absál the Fair,
Together on one Camel side by side,
Twin Kernels in a single Almond packt.
And True Love murmurs not, however small
His Chamber—nay, the straitest best of all.

When the Moon of Canaan Yúsuf

42

Darken'd in the Prison of Ægypt,
Night by Night Zulaikha went
To see him—for her Heart was broken.
Then to her said One who never
Yet had tasted of Love's Garden:
"Leavest thou thy Palace-Chamber
For the Felon's narrow Cell?"
Answer'd She, "Without my Lover,
Were my Chamber Heaven's Horizon,
It were closer than an Ant's eye;
And the Ant's eye wider were
Than Heaven, my Lover with me there!"

XIX

Six days Salámán on the Camel rode,
And then Remembrance of foregone Reproach
Abode not by him; and upon the Seventh
He halted on the Seashore, and beheld
An Ocean boundless as the Heaven above,
That, reaching its Circumference from Káf
To Káf, down to the Back of Gau and Mahi
Descended, and its Stars were Creatures' Eyes.
The Face of it was as it were a Range
Of moving Mountains; or as endless Hosts
Of Camels trooping from all Quarters up,
Furious, with the Foam upon their Lips.
In it innumerable glittering Fish
Like Jewels polish-sharp, to the sharp Eye
But for an Instant visible, glancing through
As Silver Scissors slice a blue Brocade;
Though were the Dragon from its Hollow roused,
The Dragon of the Stars would stare Aghast.
Salámán eyed the Sea, and cast about
To cross it—and forthwith upon the Shore
Devis'd a Shallop like a Crescent Moon,
Wherein that Sun and Moon in happy Hour,
Enter'd as into some Celestial Sign;
That, figured like a Bow, but Arrow-like
In Flight, was feather'd with a little Sail,

And, pitcht upon the Water like a Duck,
So with her Bosom sped to her Desire.
When they had sail'd their Vessel for a Moon,
And marr'd their Beauty with the wind o' th' Sea,
Suddenly in mid Sea reveal'd itself
An Isle, beyond Description beautiful
An Isle that all was Garden; not a Bird
Of Note or Plume in all the World but there;
There as in Bridal Retinue array'd
The Pheasant in his Crown, the Dove in her Collar;
And those who tuned their Bills among the Trees
That Arm in Arm from Fingers paralyz'd
With any Breath of Air Fruit moist and dry
Down scatter'd in Profusion to their Feet,
Where Fountains of Sweet Water ran, and round
Sunshine and Shadow chequer-chased the Ground.
Here Iram Garden seemed in Secresy
Blowing the Rosebud of its Revelation;
Or Paradise, forgetful of the Day
Of Audit, lifted from her Face the Veil.

Salámán saw the Isle, and thought no more
Of Further—there with Absál he sat down,
Absál and he together side by side
Rejoicing like the Lily and the Rose,
Together like the Body and the Soul.
Under its Trees in one another's Arms
They slept—they drank its Fountains hand in hand—
Sought Sugar with the Parrot—or in Sport
Paraded with the Peacock—raced the Partridge—
Or fell a-talking with the Nightingale.
There was the Rose without a Thorn, and there
The Treasure and no Serpent to beware—
What sweeter than your Mistress at your side
In such a Solitude, and none to Chide!

Whisper'd one to Wámik—"Oh Thou
Victim of the Wound of Azra,
What is it that like a Shadow
Movest thou about in Silence

44

Meditating Night and Day?"
Wámik answered, "Even this—
To fly with Azra to the Desert;
There by so remote a Fountain
That, whichever way one travell'd
League on League, one yet should never,
Never meet the Face of Man—
There to pitch my Tent—for ever
There to gaze on my Belovéd;
Gaze, till Gazing out of Gazing
Grew to Being Her I gaze on,
She and I no more, but in One.
Undivided Being blended,
All that is not One must ever
Suffer with the Wound of Absence;
And whoever in Love's City
Enters, finds but Room for One,
And but in Oneness Union."

XX

When by and bye The Shah was made aware
Of that Soul-wasting absence of his Son,
He reach'd a Cry to Heav'n—his Eyelashes
Wept Blood—Search everywhere he set a-foot,
But none could tell the hidden Mystery.
Then bade he bring a Mirror that he had,
A Mirror, like the Bosom of the wise,
Reflecting all the World, and lifting up
The Veil from all its Secret, Good and Evil.
That Mirror bade he bring, and, in its Face
Looking, beheld the Face of his Desire.
He saw those Lovers in the Solitude,
Turn'd from the World, and all its ways, and People,
And looking only in each other's Eyes,
And never finding any Sorrow there.
The Shah beheld them as they were, and Pity
Fell on his Eyes, and he reproach'd them not;
And, gathering all their Life into his Hand,
Not a Thread lost, disposed in Order all.

45

Oh for the Noble Nature, and Clear Heart,
That, seeing Two who draw one Breath together
Drinking the Cup of Happiness and Tears
Unshatter'd by the Stone of Separation,
Is loath their sweet Communion to destroy,
Or cast a Tangle in the Skein of Joy.

The Arrows that assail the Lords of Sorrow
Come from the Hand of Retribution.
Do Well, that in thy Turn Well may betide Thee;
And turn from Ill, that Ill may turn beside Thee.

    Firhád, Moulder of the Mountain,
    Love-distracted looked to Shírín,
    And Shírín the Sculptor's Passion
    Saw, and turn'd her Heart to Him.

    Then the Fire of Jealous Frenzy
    Caught and carried up the Harvest
    Of the Might of Kai Khusrau.

    Plotting with that ancient Hag
    Of Fate, the Sculptor's Cup he poison'd
    And remained the Lord of Love.

    So—But Fate that Fate avenges
    Arms Shirúeh with the Dagger,
    That at once from Shírín tore him,
    Hurl'd him from the Throne of Glory.

XXI

But as the days went on, and still The Shah
Beheld Salámán how sunk in Absál,
And yet no Hand of better Effort lifted;
But still the Crown that shall adorn his Head,
And still the Throne that waited for his Foot,
Trampled from Memory by a Base Desire,
Of which the Soul was still unsatisfied—
Then from the Sorrow of The Shah fell Fire;

To Gracelessness Ungracious he became,
And, quite to shatter his rebellious Lust,
Upon Salámán all his Will discharged.
And Lo! Salámán to his Mistress turn'd,
But could not reach her—look'd and look'd again,
And palpitated tow'rd her—but in Vain!
Oh Misery! what to the Bankrupt worse
Than Gold he cannot reach! To one Athirst
Than Fountain to the Eye and Lip forbid!—
Or than Heaven opened to the Eyes in Hell!—
Yet, when Salámán's Anguish was extreme,
The Door of Mercy open'd in his Face;
He saw and knew his Father's Hand outstretcht
To lift him from Perdition—timidly,
Timidly tow'rd his Father's Face his own
He lifted, Pardon-pleading, Crime-confest,
As the stray Bird one day will find her Nest.

> A Disciple ask'd a Master,
> "By what Token should a Father
> Vouch for his reputed Son?"
> Said the Master, "By the Stripling,
> Howsoever Late or Early,
> Like to the Reputed Father
> Growing—whether Wise or Foolish.
>
> "Lo the disregarded Darnel
> With itself adorns the Wheat-field,
> And for all the Early Season
> Satisfies the Farmer's Eye;
> But come once the Hour of Harvest.
> And another Grain shall answer,
> 'Darnel and no Wheat, am I.'"

XXII

When The Shah saw Salámán's face again,
And breath'd the Breath of Reconciliation,
He laid the Hand of Love upon his Shoulder,
The Kiss of Welcome on his Cheek, and said,

"Oh Thou, who lost, Love's Banquet lost its Salt,
And Mankind's Eye its Pupil!—Thy Return
Is as another Sun to Heaven; a new
Rose blooming in the Garden of the Soul.
Arise, Oh Moon of Majesty unwaned!
The Court of the Horizon is thy Court,
Thy Kingdom is the Kingdom of the World!—
Lo! Throne and Crown await Thee—Throne and Crown
Without thy Impress but uncurrent Gold,
Not to be stamp'd by one not worthy Them;
Behold! The Rebel's Face is at thy Door;
Let him not triumph—let the Wicked dread
The Throne under thy Feet, the Crown upon thy Head.
Oh Spurn them not behind Thee! Oh my Son,
Wipe Thou the Woman's Henna from thy Hand:
Withdraw Thee from the Minion who from Thee
Dominion draws; the Time is come to choose,
Thy Mistress or the World to hold or lose."
Four are the Signs of Kingly Aptitude;
Wise Head—clean Heart—strong Arm—and open Hand.
Wise is He not—Continent cannot be—
Who binds himself to an unworthy Lust;
Nor Valiant, who submits to a weak Woman;
Nor Liberal, who cannot draw his Hand
From that in which so basely he is busied.
And of these Four who misses All or One
Is not the Bridegroom of Dominion.

XXIII

Ah the poor Lover!—In the changing Hands
Of Day and Night no wretcheder than He!
No Arrow from the Bow of Evil Fate
But reaches him—one Dagger at his Throat,
Another comes to wound him from behind.
Wounded by Love—then wounded by Reproof
Of Loving—and, scarce stauncht the Blood of Shame
By flying from his Love—then, worst of all,
Love's back-blow of Revenge for having fled!

48

Salámán heard—he rent the Robe of Peace—
He came to loathe his Life, and long for Death,
(For better Death itself than Life in Death)—
He turn'd his face with Absál to the Desert—
Enter'd the deadly Plain; Branch upon Branch
Cut down, and gather'd in a lofty Pile,
And fired. They look'd upon the Flames, those Two—
They look'd, and they rejoiced; and hand in hand
They sprang into the Fire. The Shah who saw
In secret all had order'd; and the Flame,
Directed by his Self-fulfilling Will,
Devouring utterly Absál, pass'd by
Salámán harmless—the pure Gold return'd
Entire, but all the baser Metal burn'd.

XXIV

Heaven's Dome is but a wondrous House of Sorrow,
And Happiness therein a lying Fable.
When first they mix'd the Clay of Man, and cloth'd
His Spirit in the Robe of Perfect Beauty,
For Forty Mornings did an Evil Cloud
Rain Sorrows over him from Head to Foot;
And when the Forty Mornings pass'd to Night,
Then came one Morning-Shower—one Morning-Shower
Of Joy—to Forty of the Rain of Sorrow!—
And though the better Fortune came at last
To seal the Work, yet every Wise Man knows
Such Consummation never can be here!

Salámán fired the Pile; and in the Flame
That, passing him, consumed Absál like Straw,
Died his Divided Self, and there survived
His Individual; and, like a Body
From which the Soul is parted, all alone.
Then rose his Cry to Heaven—his Eyelashes
Dropt Blood—his Sighs stood like a Smoke in Heaven,
And Morning rent her Garment at his Anguish.
He tore his Bosom with his Nails—he smote
Stone on his Bosom—looking then on hands

49

No longer lockt in hers, and lost their Jewel,
He tore them with his Teeth. And when came Night,
He hid him in some Corner of the House,
And communed with the Fantom of his Love.
"Oh Thou whose Presence so long sooth'd my Soul,
Now burnt with thy Remembrance! Oh so long
The Light that fed these Eyes now dark with Tears!
Oh Long, Long Home of Love now lost for Ever!
We were Together—that was all Enough—
We two rejoicing in each other's Eyes,
Infinitely rejoicing—all the World
Nothing to Us, nor We to all the World—
No Road to reach us, nor an Eye to watch—
All Day we whisper'd in each other's Ears,
All Night we slept in one another's Arms—
All seem'd to our Desire, as if the Hand
Of unjust Fortune were for once too short.
Oh would to God that when I lit the Pyre
The Flame had left Thee Living and me Dead,
Not Living worse than Dead, depriv'd of Thee!
Oh were I but with Thee!—at any Cost
Stript of this terrible Self-solitude!
Oh but with Thee Annihilation—lost,
Or in Eternal Intercourse renew'd!"

> Slumber-drunk an Arab in the
> Desert off his Camel tumbled,
> Who the lighter of her Burden
> Ran upon her road rejoicing.
> When the Arab woke at morning,
> Rubb'd his Eyes and look'd about him—
> "Oh my Camel! Oh my Camel!"
> Quoth he, "Camel of my Soul!—
> That Lost with Her I lost might be,
> Or found, She might be found with Me!"

XXV

When in this Plight The Shah Salámán saw,
His Soul was struck with Anguish, and the Vein

50

Of Life within was strangled—what to do
He knew not. Then he turn'd him to The Sage—
"On Altar of the World, to whom Mankind
Directs the Face of Prayer in Weal or Woe,
Nothing but Wisdom can untie the Knot;
And art not Thou the Wisdom of the World,
The Master-Key of all its Difficulties?
Absál is perisht; and, because of Her,
Salámán dedicates his Life to Sorrow;
I cannot bring back Her, nor comfort Him.
Lo, I have said! My Sorrow is before Thee;
From thy far-reaching Wisdom help Thou Me
Fast in the Hand of Sorrow! Help Thou Me,
For I am very wretched!" Then The Sage—
"Oh Thou that err'st not from the Road of Right,
If but Salámán have not broke my Bond,
Nor lies beyond the Noose of my Firmán,
He quickly shall unload his Heart to me,
And I will find a Remedy for all."

XXVI

Then The Sage counsell'd, and Salámán heard,
And drew the Wisdom down into his Heart;
And, sitting in the Shadow of the Perfect,
His Soul found Quiet under; sweet it seem'd,
Sweeping the Chaff and Litter from his own,
To be the very Dust of Wisdom's Door,
Slave of the Firmán of the Lord of Life,
Then The Sage marvell'd at his Towardness,
And wrought in Miracle in his behalf.
He pour'd the Wine of Wisdom in his Cup,
He laid the Dew of Peace upon his lips;
And when Old Love return'd to Memory,
And broke in Passion from his Lips, The Sage
Under whose waxing Will Existence rose
Responsive, and, relaxing, waned again,
Raising a Fantom Image of Absál
Set it awhile before Salámán's Eyes,
Till, having sow'd the Seed of Quiet there,

It went again down to Annihilation.
But ever, for the Sum of his Discourse,
The Sage would tell of a Celestial Love;
"Zuhrah," he said, "the Lustre of the Stars—
'Fore whom the Beauty of the Brightest wanes;
Who were she to reveal her perfect Beauty,
The Sun and Moon would craze; Zuhrah," he said,
"The Sweetness of the Banquet—none in Song
Like Her—her Harp filling the Ear of Heaven,
That Dervish-dances at her Harmony."
Salámán listen'd, and inclin'd—again
Repeated, Inclination ever grew;
Until The Sage beholding in his Soul
The Spirit quicken, so effectually
With Zuhrah wrought, that she reveal'd herself
In her pure Beauty to Salámán's Soul,
And washing Absál's Image from his Breast,
There reign'd instead. Celestial Beauty seen,
He left the Earthly; and, once come to know
Eternal Love, he let the Mortal go.

XXVII

The Crown of Empire how supreme a Lot!
The Throne of the Sultán how high!—But not
For All—None but the Heaven-ward Foot may dare
To mount—The Head that touches Heaven to wear!—

When the Belov'd of Royal Augury
Was rescued from the Bondage of Absál,
Then he arose, and shaking off the Dust
Of that lost Travel, girded up his Heart,
And look'd with undefiléd Robe to Heaven.
Then was His Head worthy to wear the Crown,
His Foot to mount the Throne. And then The Shah
Summon'd the Chiefs of Cities and of States,
Summon'd the Absolute Ones who wore the Ring,
And such a Banquet order'd as is not
For Sovereign Assemblement the like
In the Folding of the Records of the World.

No arméd Host, nor Captain of a Host,
From all the Quarters of the World, but there;
Of whom not one but to Salámán did
Obeisance, and lifted up his Neck
To yoke it under his Supremacy.
Then The Shah crown'd him with the Golden Crown,
And set the Golden Throne beneath his Feet.
And over all the Heads of the Assembly,
And in the Ears of all of them, his Jewels
With the Diamond of Wisdom cut and said:—

XXVIII

"My Son, the Kingdom of The World is not
Eternal, nor the Sum of right Desire;
Make thou the Faith-preserving Intellect
Thy Counsellor; and considering To-day
To-morrow's Seed-field, ere That come to bear,
Sow with the Harvest of Eternity.
All Work with Wisdom hath to do—by that
Stampt current only; what Thyself to do
Art wise, that *Do*; what not, consult the Wise,
Turn not thy Face away from the old Ways,
That were the Canon of the Kings of Old;
Nor cloud with Tyranny the Glass of Justice;
But rather strive that all Confusion
Change by thy Justice to its opposite.
In whatsoever Thou shalt Take or Give
Look to the *How*; Giving and Taking still,
Not by the backward Counsel of the Godless,
But by the Law of Faith increase and Give.
Drain not thy People's purse—the Tyranny
Which Thee enriches at thy Subjects' cost,
Awhile shall make Thee strong; but in the End
Shall bow thy Neck beneath a Double Burden.
The Tyrant goes to Hell—follow not Him—

"Become not Thou the Fuel of its Fires.
Thou art a Shepherd, and thy Flock the People,
To save and not destroy; nor at their Loss

53

To lift Thyself above the Shepherd's calling.
For which is for the other, Flock or Shepherd?
And join with Thee true Men to keep the Flock.
Dogs, if you will—but Trusty—head in leash,
Whose Teeth are for the Wolf, not for the Lamb,
And least of all the Wolf's Accomplices,
Their Jaws blood-dripping from the Tyrant's Shambles.
For Shahs must have Vizírs—but be they Wise
And Trusty—knowing well the Realm's Estate—
(For who eats Profit of a Fool? and least
A wise King girdled by a Foolish Council)—
Knowing how far to Shah and Subject bound
On either Hand—not by Extortion,
Nor Usury wrung from the People's purse,
Their Master's and their own Estates (to whom
Enough is apt enough to make them Rebel)
Feeding to such a Surplus as feeds Hell.
Proper in Soul and Body be They—pitiful
To Poverty—hospitable to the Saint—
Their sweet Access a Salve to wounded Hearts,
Their Vengeance terrible to the Evil Doer,
Thy Heralds through the Country bringing Thee
Report of Good or Ill—which to confirm
By thy peculiar Eye—and least of all
Suffering Accuser also to be Judge—
By surest Steps builds up Prosperity."

XXIX

EPILOGUE

Under the Outward Form of any Story
An Inner Meaning lies—This Story now
Completed, do Thou of its Mystery
(Whereto the Wise hath found himself a way)
Have thy Desire—No Tale of I and Thou,
Though I and Thou be its Interpreters.
What signifies The Shah? and what the Sage?
And what Salámán not of Woman born?
And what Absál who drew him to Desire?

54

And what the Kingdom that awaited him
When he had drawn his Garment from her Hand?
What means that Fiery Pile? and what The Sea?
And what that Heavenly Zuhrah who at last
Clear'd Absál from the Mirror of his Soul?
Learn part by part the Mystery from me;
All Ear from Head to Foot and Understanding be.

XXX

The Incomparable Creator, when this World
He did create, created First of All
The First Intelligence—First of a Chain
Of Ten Intelligences, of which the Last
Sole Agent is in this our Universe,
Active Intelligence so call'd; The One
Distributor of Evil and of Good,
Of Joy and Sorrow, Himself apart from Matter,
In Essence and in Energy—his Treasure
Subject to no such Talisman—He yet
Hath fashion'd all that is—Material Form,
And Spiritual, sprung from Him—by Him
Directed all, and in his Bounty drown'd.
Therefore is He that Firmán-issuing Shah
To whom the World was subject. But because
What He distributes to the Universe
Himself from still a Higher Power receives,
The Wise, and all who comprehend aright,
Will recognise that Higher in The Sage.
His the Prime Spirit that, spontaneously
Projected by the Tenth Intelligence,
Was from no Womb of Matter reproduced
A Special Essence called The Soul—a Child
Fresh sprung from Heaven in Raiment undefiled
Of Sensual Taint, and therefore call'd Salámán.
And who Absál?—The Lust-adoring Body,
Slave to the Blood and Sense—through whom The Soul,
Although the Body's very Life it be,
Does yet imbibe the Knowledge and Desire
Of Things of Sense; and these united thus

55

By such a Tie God only can unloose,
Body and Soul are Lovers Each of other.

What is The Sea on which they sail'd?—The Sea
Of Animal Desire—the Sensual Abyss,
Under whose Waters lie a World of Being
Swept far from God in that Submersion.

And wherefore was it Absál in that Isle
Deceived in her Delight, and that Salámán
Fell short of his Desire?—That was to show
How Passion tires, and how with Time begins
The Folding of the Carpet of Desire.
And what the turning of Salámán's Heart
Back to the Shah, and looking to the Throne
Of Pomp and Glory? What but the Return
Of the Lost Soul to its true Parentage,
And back from Carnal Error looking up
Repentant to its Intellectual Throne.
What is The Fire?—Ascetic Discipline,
That burns away the Animal Alloy,
Till all the Dross of Matter be consumed,
And the Essential Soul, its Raiment clean
Of Mortal Taint, be left. But forasmuch
As any Life-long Habit so consumed,
May well recur a Pang for what is lost,
Therefore The Sage set in Salámán's Eyes
A Soothing Fantom of the Past, but still
Told of a Better Venus, till his Soul
She fill'd, and blotted out his Mortal Love.
For what is Zuhrah?—That Divine Perfection,
Wherewith the Soul inspir'd and all array'd
In Intellectual Light is Royal blest,
And mounts The Throne and wears The Crown, and
     Reigns
Lord of the Empire of Humanity.

This is the Meaning of This Mystery
Which to know wholly ponder in thy Heart,
Till all its ancient Secret be enlarged.

Enough—The written Summary I close,
And set my Seal:

The Truth God only Knows

PERSIAN POETRY

AN ESSAY BY RALPH WALDO EMERSON

To Baron Von Hammer-Purgstall, who died in Vienna in 1856, we owe our best knowledge of the Persians. He has translated into German, besides the "Divan" of Hafiz, specimens of two hundred poets, who wrote during a period of five and a half centuries, from A.D. 1050 to 1600. The seven masters of the Persian Parnassus—Firdousi, Enweri, Nisami, Dschelaleddin, Saadi, Hafiz, and Dschami—have ceased to be empty names; and others, like Ferideddin Attar and Omar Chiam, promise to rise in Western estimation. That for which mainly books exist is communicated in these rich extracts. Many qualities go to make a good telescope,—as the largeness of the field, facility of sweeping the meridian, achromatic purity of lenses, and so forth,—but the one eminent value is the space penetrating power; and there are many virtues in books,—but the essential value is the adding of knowledge to our stock, by the record of new facts, and, better, by the record of intuitions, which distribute facts, and are the formulas which supersede all histories.

Oriental life and society, especially in the Southern nations, stand in violent contrast with the multitudinous detail, the secular stability, and the vast average of comfort of the Western nations. Life in the East is fierce, short, hazardous, and in extremes. Its elements are few and simple, not exhibiting the long range and undulation of European existence, but rapidly reaching the best and the worst. The rich feed on fruits and game,—the poor on a watermelon's peel. All or nothing is the genius of Oriental life. Favour of the Sultan, or his displeasure, is a question of Fate. A war is undertaken for an epigram or a distich, as in Europe for a duchy. The prolific sun, and the sudden and rank plenty which his heat engenders, make subsistence easy. On the other side, the desert, the simoom, the mirage, the lion, and the plague endanger it, and life hangs on the contingency of a skin of water more or less. The very geography of old Persia showed these contrasts. "My father's empire," said Cyrus to Xenophon, "is so large, that people perish with cold, at one extremity, whilst they are suffocated with heat, at the other." The temperament of the people agrees with this life in extremes. Religion and poetry are all their civilization. The religion teaches an inexorable Destiny. It distinguishes only two days in each man's history—his birthday, called *the Day of the Lot,* and the Day of Judgment. Courage and absolute submission to what is appointed him are his virtues.

The favour of the climate making subsistence easy and encouraging an outdoor life, allows to the Eastern nations a highly intellectual organization,—leaving out of view, at present, the genius of the Hindoos (more Oriental in every sense), whom no people have surpassed in the grandeur of their ethical statement. The Persians and the Arabs, with great leisure and few books, are exquisitely sensible to the pleasures of poetry. Layard has given some details of the effect which the *improvvisatori* produced on the children of the desert. "When the bard improvised an amatory ditty, the young chief's excitement was almost beyond control. The other Bedouins were scarcely less moved by these rude measures, which have the same kind of effect on the wild tribes of the Persian mountains. Such verses, chanted by their self-taught poets, or by the girls of their encampment, will drive warriors to the combat, fearless of death, or prove an ample reward, on their return from the dangers of the *ghazon*, or the fight. The excitement they produce exceeds that of the grape. He who would understand the influence of the Homeric ballads in the heroic ages should witness the effect which similar compositions have upon the wild nomads of the East." Elsewhere he adds, "Poetry and flowers are the wine and spirits of the Arab; a couplet is equal to a bottle, and a rose to a dram, without the evil effect of either."

The Persian poetry rests on a mythology whose few legends are connected with the Jewish history, and the anterior traditions of the Pentateuch. The principal figure in the allusions of Eastern poetry is Solomon. Solomon had three talismans; first, the signet-ring, by which he commanded the spirits, on the stone of which was engraven the name of God; second, the glass, in which he saw the secrets of his enemies, and the causes of all things, figured; the third, the east-wind, which was his horse. His counsellor was Simorg, king of birds, the all-wise fowl, who had lived ever since the beginning of the world, and now lives alone on the highest summit of Mount Kaf. No fowler has taken him, and none now living has seen him. By him Solomon was taught the language of birds, so that he heard secrets whenever he went into his gardens. When Solomon travelled, the throne was placed on a carpet of green silk, of a length and breadth sufficient for all his army to stand upon,—men placing themselves on his right hand, and the spirits on his left. When all were in order, the east-wind, at his command, took up the carpet and transported it, with all that were upon it, whither he pleased,—the army of birds at the same time flying overhead, and forming a canopy to shade them from the sun. It is related that when the Queen of Sheba came to visit Solomon, he had built, against her arrival, a palace, of which the floor or pavement was of glass, laid over running water, in which fish were swimming. The Queen of Sheba was deceived thereby, and raised her robes, thinking she was to pass through the water. On the occasion of Solomon's marriage, all the beasts, laden with presents, appeared before his throne. Behind them all came the ant, with a blade of grass: Solomon did not despise the gift of the ant. Asaph, the vizier, at a certain time, lost the seal of Solomon, which one of the Dews, or evil spirits, found, and, governing in the name of Solomon, deceived the people.

Firdousi, the Persian Homer, has written in the *Shah Nameh* the annals of the fabulous and heroic kings of the country: of Karum (the Persian Croesus), the immeasurably rich gold-maker, who, with all his treasures, lies buried not far from the Pyramids, in the sea which bears his name; of Jamschid, the binder of demons, whose reign lasted seven hundred years; of Kai Kaus, in whose palace, built by demons on Alburz, gold and silver and precious stones were used so lavishly, that in the brilliancy produced by their combined effect, night and day appeared the same; of Afrasiyab, strong as an elephant, whose shadow extended for miles, whose heart was bounteous as the ocean, and his hands like the clouds when rain falls to gladden the earth. The crocodile in the rolling stream had no safety from Afrasiyab. Yet when he came to fight against the generals of Kaus, he was but an insect in the grasp of Rustem, who seized him by the girdle, and dragged him from his horse. Rustem felt such anger at the arrogance of the King of Mazinderan, that every hair on his body started up like a spear. The gripe of his hand cracked the sinews of an enemy.

These legends,—with Chiser, the fountain of life, Tuba, the tree of life,—the romances of the loves of Leila and Medschun, of Chosru and Schirin, and those of the nightingale for the rose,—pearl-diving, and the virtues of gems,—the cohol, the cosmetic by which pearls and eyebrows are indelibly stained black,—the bladder in which musk is brought,—the down of the lip, the mole on the cheek, the eyelash,—lilies, roses, tulips and jasmines,—make the staple imagery of Persian odes.

The Persians have epics and tales, but, for the most part, they affect short poems and epigrams. Gnomic verses, rules of life conveyed in a lively image, especially in an image addressed to the eye, and contained in a single stanza, were always current in the East; and if the poem is long, it is only a string of unconnected verses. They use an inconsecutiveness quite alarming to Western logic, and the connection between the stanzas of their longer odes is much like that between the refrain of our old English ballads,

"The sun shines fair on Carlisle wall,"

or

"The rain it raineth every day,"

and the main story.

Take, as specimens of these gnomic verses, the following:—

"The secret that should not be blown
Not one of thy nation must know;
You may padlock the gate of a town,
But never the mouth of a foe."

Or this of Omar Chiam:—

"On earth's wide thoroughfares below
Two only men contented go:
Who knows what's right and what's forbid,
And he from whom is knowledge hid."

Here is a poem on a melon, by Adsched of Meru:—

"Colour, taste, and smell, smaragdus, sugar and musk,—
Amber for the tongue, for the eye a picture rare,—
If you cut the fruit in slices, every slice a crescent fair,—
If you leave it whole, the full harvest moon is there."

62

Hafiz is the prince of Persian poets, and in his extraordinary gifts adds to some of the attributes of Pindar, Anacreon, Horace, and Burns the insight of a mystic, that sometimes affords a deeper glance at Nature than belongs to either of these bards. He accosts all topics with an easy audacity. "He only," he says, "is fit for company, who knows how to prize earthly happiness at the value of a nightcap. Our father Adam sold Paradise for two kernels of wheat; then blame me not if I hold it dear at one grapestone." He says to the Shah, "Thou who rulest after words and thoughts which no ear has heard and no mind has thought, abide firm until thy young destiny tears off his blue coat from the old graybeard of the sky." He says:—

> "I batter the wheel of heaven
> When it rolls not rightly by;
> I am not one of the snivellers,
> Who fall thereon and die."

The rapidity of his turns is always surprising us:—

> "See how the roses burn!
> Bring wine to quench the fire!
> Alas! the flames come up with us,—
> We perish with desire."

After the manner of his nation, he abounds in pregnant sentences which might be engraved on a sword-blade and almost on a ring. "In honour dies he to whom the great seems ever wonderful." "Here is the sum, that, when one door opens, another shuts." "On every side is an ambush laid by the robber-troops of circumstance; hence it is that the horseman of life urges on his courser at headlong speed." "The earth is a host who murders his guests." "Good is what goes on the road of Nature. On the straight way the traveller never misses."

> "Alas! till now I had not known
> My guide and Fortune's guide are one."

63

"The understanding's copper coin
Counts not with the gold of love."

"'Tis writ on Paradise's gate,
'Woe to the dupe that yields to Fate!'"

"The world is a bride superbly dressed;
Who weds her for dowry must pay his soul."

"Loose the knots of the heart; never think on thy fate;
No Euclid has yet disentangled that snarl."

"There resides in the grieving
A poison to kill;
Beware to go near them,
'Tis pestilent still."

Harems and wine-shops only give him a new ground of
observation, whence to draw sometimes a deeper moral
than regulated sober life affords,—and this is foreseen:—

"I will be drunk and down with wine;
Treasures we find in a ruined house."

Riot, he thinks, can snatch from the deeply hidden lot the
veil that covers it:—

"To be wise the dull brain so earnestly throbs,
Bring bands of wine for the stupid head."

"The Builder of heaven
Hath sundered the earth,
So that no footway
Leads out of it forth.

"On turnpikes of wonder
Wine leads the mind forth,
Straight, sidewise, and upward,
West, southward, and north.

"Stands the vault adamantine
Until the Doomsday;
The wine-cup shall ferry
Thee o'er it away."

That hardihood and self-equality of every sound nature, which result from the feeling that the spirit in him is entire and as good as the world, which entitle the poet to speak with authority, and make him an object of interest, and his every phrase and syllable significant, are in Hafiz, and abundantly fortify and ennoble his tone.

His was the fluent mind in which every thought and feeling came readily to the lips. "Loose the knots of the heart," he says. We absorb elements enough, but have not leaves and lungs for healthy perspiration and growth. An air of sterility, of incompetence to their proper aims, belongs to many who have both experience and wisdom. But a large utterance, a river that makes its own shores, quick perception and corresponding expression, a constitution to which every morrow is a new day, which is equal to the needs of life, at once tender and bold, with great arteries,—this generosity of ebb and flow satisfies, and we should be willing to die when our time comes, having had our swing and gratification. The difference is not so much in the quality of men's thoughts as in the power of uttering them. What is pent and smouldered in the dumb actor is not pent in the poet, but passes over into new form, at once relief and creation.

The other merit of Hafiz is his intellectual liberty, which is a certificate of profound thought. We accept the religions and politics into which we fall; and it is only a few delicate spirits who are sufficient to see that the whole web of convention is the imbecility of those whom it entangles,— that the mind suffers no religion and no empire but its own. It indicates this respect to absolute truth by the use it makes of the symbols that are most stable and reverend, and therefore is always provoking the accusation of irreligion.

65

Hypocrisy is the perpetual butt of his arrows.

"Let us draw the cowl through the brook of wine."

He tells his mistress that not the dervis, or the monk, but the lover, has in his heart the spirit which makes the ascetic and the saint; and certainly not their cowls and mummeries, but her glances, can impart to him the fire and virtue needful for such self-denial. Wrong shall not be wrong to Hafiz, for the name's sake. A law or statute is to him what a fence is to a nimble school-boy,—a temptation for a jump. "We would do nothing but good, else would shame come to us on the day when the soul must hie hence; and should they then deny us Paradise, the Houris themselves would forsake that, and come out to us."

His complete intellectual emancipation he communicates to the reader. There is no example of such facility of allusion, such use of all materials. Nothing is too high, nothing too low, for his occasion. He fears nothing, he stops for nothing. Love is a leveller, and Allah becomes a groom, and heaven a closet, in his daring hymns to his mistress or to his cupbearer. This boundless charter is the right of genius.

We do not wish to strew sugar on bottled spiders, or try to make mystical divinity out of the Song of Solomon, much less out of the erotic and bacchanalian songs of Hafiz. Hafiz himself is determined to defy all such hypocritical interpretation, and tears off his turban and throws it at the head of the meddling dervis, and throws his glass after the turban. But the love or the wine of Hafiz is not to be confounded with vulgar debauch. It is the spirit in which the song is written that imports, and not the topics. Hafiz praises wine, roses, maidens, boys, birds, mornings, and music, to give vent to his immense hilarity and sympathy with every form of beauty and joy; and lays the emphasis on these to mark his scorn of sanctimony and base prudence. These are the natural topics and language of his wit and perception. But it is the play of wit and the joy

66

of song that he loves; and if you mistake him for a low rioter, he turns short on you with verses which express the poverty of sensual joys, and to ejaculate with equal fire the most unpalatable affirmations of heroic sentiment and contempt for the world. Sometimes it is a glance from the height of thought, as thus:—"Bring wine; for, in the audience-hall of the soul's independence, what is sentinel or Sultan? what is the wise man or the intoxicated?" And sometimes his feast, feasters, and world are only one pebble more in the eternal vortex and revolution of Fate:—

> "I am; what I am
> My dust will be again."

A saint might lend an ear to the riotous fun of Falstaff; for it is not created to excite the animal appetites, but to vent the joy of a supernal intelligence. In all poetry, Pindar's rule holds,—συνετοῖς φωνεί, it speaks to the intelligent; and Hafiz is a poet for poets, whether he write, as sometimes, with a parrot's, or, as at other times, with an eagle's quill.

Every song of Hafiz affords new proof of the unimportance of your subject to success, provided only the treatment be cordial. In general, what is more tedious than dedications or panegyrics addressed to grandees? Yet in the "Divan" you would not skip them, since his muse seldom supports him better.

> "What lovelier forms things wear,
> Now that the Shah comes back!"

And again:—

> "Thy foes to hunt, thy enviers to strike down,
> Poises Arcturus aloft morning and evening his spear."

It is told of Hafiz, that, when he had written a compliment to a handsome youth,—

"Take my heart in thy hand, O beautiful boy of
    Shiraz!
  I would give for the mole on thy cheek Samarcand
    and Buchara!"—

the verses came to the ear of Timour in his palace. Timour
taxed Hafiz with treating disrespectfully his two cities, to
raise and adorn which he had conquered nations. Hafiz
replied, "Alas, my lord, if I had not been so prodigal, I had
not been so poor!"

The Persians had a mode of establishing copyright the
most secure of any contrivance with which we are
acquainted. The law of the *ghaselle*, or shorter ode,
requires that the poet insert his name in the last stanza.
Almost every one of several hundreds of poems of Hafiz
contains his name thus interwoven more or less closely
with the subject of the piece. It is itself a test of skill, as
this self-naming is not quite easy. We remember but two
or three examples in English poetry; that of Chaucer, in
the "House of Fame": Jonson's epitaph on his son,—

"Ben Jonson his best piece of poetry":

and Cowley's,—

"The melancholy Cowley lay."

But it is easy to Hafiz. It gives him the opportunity of the
most playful self-assertion, always gracefully, sometimes
almost in the fun of Falstaff, sometimes with feminine
delicacy. He tells us, "The angels in heaven were lately
learning his last pieces." He says, "The fishes shed their
pearls, out of desire and longing as soon as the ship of
Hafiz swims the deep."

"Out of the East, out of the West, no man
    understands me;

68

O, the happier I, who confide to none but the
   wind!
This morning heard I how the lyre of the stars
   resounded,
'Sweeter tones have we heard from Hafiz!'"

Again,—"I heard the harp of the planet Venus, and it said
in the early morning, 'I am the disciple of the sweet-voiced
Hafiz!'" And again,—"When Hafiz sings, the angels
hearken, and Anaitis, the leader of the starry host, calls
even the Messiah in heaven out to the dance." "No one has
unveiled thoughts like Hafiz, since the locks of the Word-
bride were first curled." "Only he despises the verse of
Hafiz who is not himself by nature noble."

But we must try to give some of these poetic flourishes the
metrical form which they seem to require:—

"Fit for the Pleiad's azure chord
The songs I sung, the pearls I bored."

Another:—

"I have no hoarded treasure,
Yet have I rich content;
The first from Allah to the Shah,
The last to Hafiz went."

Another:—

"High heart, O Hafiz! though not thine
Fine gold and silver ore;
More worth to thee the gift of song,
And the clear insight more."

Again:—

"O Hafiz speak not of thy need;
Are not these verses thine?

Then all the poets are agreed,
No man can less repine."

He asserts his dignity as bard and inspired man of his people. To the Vizier returning from Mecca, he says, "Boast not rashly, prince of pilgrims, of thy fortune. Thou hast indeed seen the temple; but I, the Lord of the temple. Nor has any man inhaled from the musk-bladder of the merchant, or from the musky morning-wind, that sweet air which I am permitted to breathe every hour of the day." And with still more vigour in the following lines:—

"Oft have I said, I say it once more,
I, a wanderer, do not stray from myself,
I am a kind of parrot; the mirror is holden to me;
What the Eternal says, I stammering say again.
Give me what you will; I eat thistles as roses,
And according to my food I grow and I give.
Scorn me not, but know I have the pearl,
And am only seeking one to receive it."

And his claim has been admitted from the first. The muleteers and camel-drivers, on their way through the desert, sing snatches of his songs, not so much for the thought, as for their joyful temper and tone; and the cultivated Persians know his poems by heart. Yet Hafiz does not appear to have set any great value on his songs, since his scholars collected them for the first time after his death.

In the following poem the soul is figured as the Phœnix alighting on Tuba, the Tree of Life:—

"My phœnix long ago secured
His nest in the sky-vault's cope;
In the body's cage immured,
He was weary of life's hope.

"Round and round this heap of ashes
Now flies the bird amain,

But in that odorous niche of heaven
Nestles the bird again.

"Once, flies he upwards, he will perch
On Tuba's golden bough;
His home is on that fruited arch
Which cools the blest below.

"If over this world of ours
His wings my phœnix spread,
How gracious falls on land and sea
The soul-refreshing shade!

"Either world inhabits he,
See oft below him planets roll;
His body is all of air compact,
Of Allah's love his soul."

Here is an ode which is said to be a favourite with all
educated Persians:—

"Come!—the palace of heaven rest on aëry pillars,—
Come, and bring me wine; our days are wind.
I declare myself the slave of that masculine soul
Which ties and alliance on earth once for ever renounces.
Told I thee yester-morn how the Iris of heaven
Brought to me in my cup a gospel of joy?
O high-flying falcon! the Tree of Life is thy perch;
This nook of grief fits thee ill for a nest.
Hearken! they call to thee down from the ramparts of
heaven;
I cannot divine what holds thee here in a net.
I, too, have a counsel for thee; O mark it and keep it.
Since I received the same from the Master above:
Seek not for faith or for truth in a world of light-minded
girls;
A thousand suitors reckons this dangerous bride.
Cumber thee not for the world, and this my precept forget
not,
'Tis but a toy that a vagabond sweetheart has left us.

71

Accept whatever befalls; uncover thy brow from thy
    locks;
Never to me nor to thee was option imparted;
Neither endurance nor truth belongs to the laugh of the
rose.
The loving nightingale mourns;—cause enow for
mourning;—
Why envies the bird the streaming verses of Hafiz?
Know that a god bestowed on him eloquent speech."

The cedar, the cypress, the palm, the olive, and fig-tree,
the birds that inhabit them, and the garden flowers, are
never wanting in these musky verses, and are always
named with effect. "The willows," he says, "bow themselves
to every wind, out of shame for their unfruitfulness." We
may open anywhere on a floral catalogue.

"By breath of beds of roses drawn,
I found the grove in the morning pure,
In the concert of the nightingales
My drunken brain to cure.

"With unrelated glance
I looked the rose in the eye:
The rose in the hour of gloaming
Flamed like a lamp hard-by.

"She was of her beauty proud.
And prouder of her youth,
The while unto her flaming heart
The bulbul gave his truth.

"The sweet narcissus closed
Its eye, with passion pressed;
The tulips out of envy burned
Moles in their scarlet breast,

"The lilies white prolonged
Their sworded tongue to the smell;
The clustering anemones

72

Their pretty secrets tell."

Presently we have,—

"All day the rain
Bathed the dark hyacinths in vain,
The flood may pour from morn till night
Nor wash the pretty Indians white."

And so onward, through many a page.

This picture of the first days of Spring, from Enweri, seems to belong to Hafiz:—

"O'er the garden water goes the wind alone
To rasp and to polish the cheek of the wave;
The fire is quenched on the dear hearthstone,
But it burns again on the tulips brave."

Friendship is a favourite topic of the Eastern poets, and they have matched on this head the absoluteness of Montaigne.

Hafiz says, "Thou learnest no secret until thou knoweth friendship; since to the unsound no heavenly knowledge enters."

Ibn Jemin writes thus:

"Whilst I disdain the populace,
I find no peer in higher place,
Friend is a word of royal tone,
Friend is a poem all alone.

"Wisdom is like the elephant,
Lofty and rare inhabitant:
He dwells in deserts or in courts;
With hucksters he has no resorts."

73

Dschami says,—

"A friend is he, who, hunted as a foe,
So much the kindlier shows him than before;
Throw stones at him, or ruder javelins throw,
He builds with stone and steel a firmer floor."

Of the amatory poetry of Hafiz we must be very sparing in
our citations, though it forms the staple of the "Divan." He
has run through the whole gamut of passion,—from the
sacred to the borders, and over the borders, of the
profane. The same confusion of high and low, the celerity
of flight and allusion which our colder muses forbid, is
habitual to him. From the plain text,—

"The chemist of love
Will this perishing mould,
Were it made out of mire,
Transmute into gold."—

he proceeds to the celebration of his passion; and nothing
in his religious or in his scientific traditions is too sacred
or too remote to afford a token of his mistress. The Moon
thought she knew her own orbit well enough; but when
she saw the curve on Zuleika's cheek, she was at a loss:—

"And since round lines are drawn
My darling's lips about,
The very Moon looks puzzled on,
And hesitates in doubt
If the sweet curve that rounds thy mouth
Be not her true way to the South."

His ingenuity never sleeps:—

"Ah could I hide me in my song,
To kiss thy lips from which it flows!"

and plays in a thousand pretty courtesies:—

"Fair fall thy soft heart!
A good work wilt thou do?
O, pray for the dead
Whom thine eyelashes slew;"

And what a nest has he found for his bonny bird to take
up her abode in!—

"They strew in the paths of kings and czars
Jewels and gems of price:
But for thy head I will pluck down stars,
And pave thy way with eyes.

"I have sought for thee a costlier dome
Than Mahmoud's palace high,
And thou, returning, find thy home
In the apple of Love's eye."

Then we have all degrees of passionate
abandonment:—

"I know this perilous love-lane
No whither the traveller leads,
Yet my fancy the sweet scent of
Thy tangled tresses feeds.

"In the midnight of thy locks,
I renounce the day;
In the ring of thy rose-lips,
My heart forgets to pray."

And sometimes his love rises to a religious sentiment:—

"Plunge in your angry waves,
Renouncing doubt and care;
The flowing of the seven broad seas
Shall never wet thy hair.

"Is Allah's face on thee
Bending with love benign,

And thou not less on Allah's eye,
O fairest turnest thine."

We add to these fragments of Hafiz a few specimens from other poets.

NISAMI

"While roses bloomed along the plain,
The nightingale to the falcon said,
'Why of all birds must thou be dumb?
With closed mouth thou utterest,
Though dying, no last word to man.
Yet sitt'st thou on the hand of princes,
And feedest on the grouse's breast,
Whilst I, who hundred thousand jewels
Squander in a single tone,
Lo! I feed myself with worms,
And my dwelling is the thorn.'—
The falcon answered, 'Be all ear:
I, experienced in affairs,
See fifty things, say never one;
But thee the people prizes not
Who, doing nothing, say'st a thousand.
To me, appointed to the chase,
The king's hand gives the grouse's breast;
Whilst a chatterer like thee
Must gnaw worms in the thorn. Farewell!'"

The following passages exhibit the strong tendency of the Persian poets to contemplative and religious poetry and to allegory.

76

ENWERI

BODY AND SOUL

"A painter in China once painted a hall;—
Such a web never hung on an emperor's wall;—
One half from his brush with rich colours did run,
The other he touched with a beam of the sun;
So that all which delighted the eye in one side,
The same, point to point, in the other replied.

"In thee, friend, that Tyrian chamber is found;
Thine the star-pointing roof, and the base on the
        ground:
Is one half depicted with colours less bright?
Beware that the counterpart blazes with light!"

IBN JEMIN

"I read on the porch of a palace bold
In a purple tablet letters cast,—
'A house though a million winters old,
A house of earth comes down at last;
Then quarry thy stones from the crystal All,
And build the dome that shall not fall.'"

"What need," cries the mystic Feisi, "of palaces and
tapestry? What need even of a bed?"

"The eternal Watcher who doth wake
All night in the body's earthen chest,
Will of thine arms a pillow make,
And a bolster of thy breast."

Ferideddin Attar wrote the "Bird Conversations," a
mystical tale in which the birds coming together to choose
their king, resolve on a pilgrimage to Mount Kaf, to pay
their homage to the Simorg. From this poem, written five
hundred years ago, we cite the following passage, as a
proof of the identity of mysticism in all periods. The tone is

quite modern. In the fable, the birds were soon weary of the length and difficulties of the way, and at last almost all gave out. Three only persevered, and arrived before the throne of the Simorg.

"The bird-soul was ashamed;
Their body was quite annihilated;
They had cleaned themselves from the dust,
And were by the light ensouled.
What was, and was not,—the Past,—
Was wiped out from their breast.
The sun from near-by beamed
Clearest light into their soul;
The resplendence of the Simorg beamed
As one back from all three.
They knew not, amazed, if they
Were either this or that.
They saw themselves all as Simorg,
Themselves in the eternal Simorg.
When to the Simorg up they looked,
They beheld him among themselves;
And when they looked on each other
They saw themselves in the Simorg.
A single look grouped the two parties,
The Simorg emerged, the Simorg vanished,
This in that, and that in this,
As the world has never heard.
So remained they, sunk in wonder,
Thoughtless in deepest thinking,
And quite unconscious of themselves.
Speechless prayed they to the Highest
To open this secret,
And to unlock *Thou* and *We*.
There came an answer without tongue.—
'The Highest is a sun-mirror;
Who comes to Him sees himself therein,
Sees body and soul, and soul and body;
When you came to the Simorg,
Three therein appeared to you,
And, had fifty of you come,

So had you seen yourselves as many.
Him has none of us yet seen.
Ants see not the Pleiades.
Can the gnat grasp with his teeth
The body of the elephant?
What you see is He not;
What you hear is He not.
The valleys which you traverse,
The actions which you perform,
They lie under our treatment
And among our properties
You as three birds are amazed,
Impatient, heartless, confused:
Far over you am I raised,
Since I am in act Simorg.
Ye blot out my highest being,
That ye may find yourselves on my throne;
For ever ye blot out yourselves,
As shadows in the sun. Farewell!'"

www.ingramcontent.com/pod-product-compliance
Lightning Source LLC
Chambersburg PA
CBHW010237100426
42813CB00041B/3478/J